D0968966

A BOOK OF PREFACES

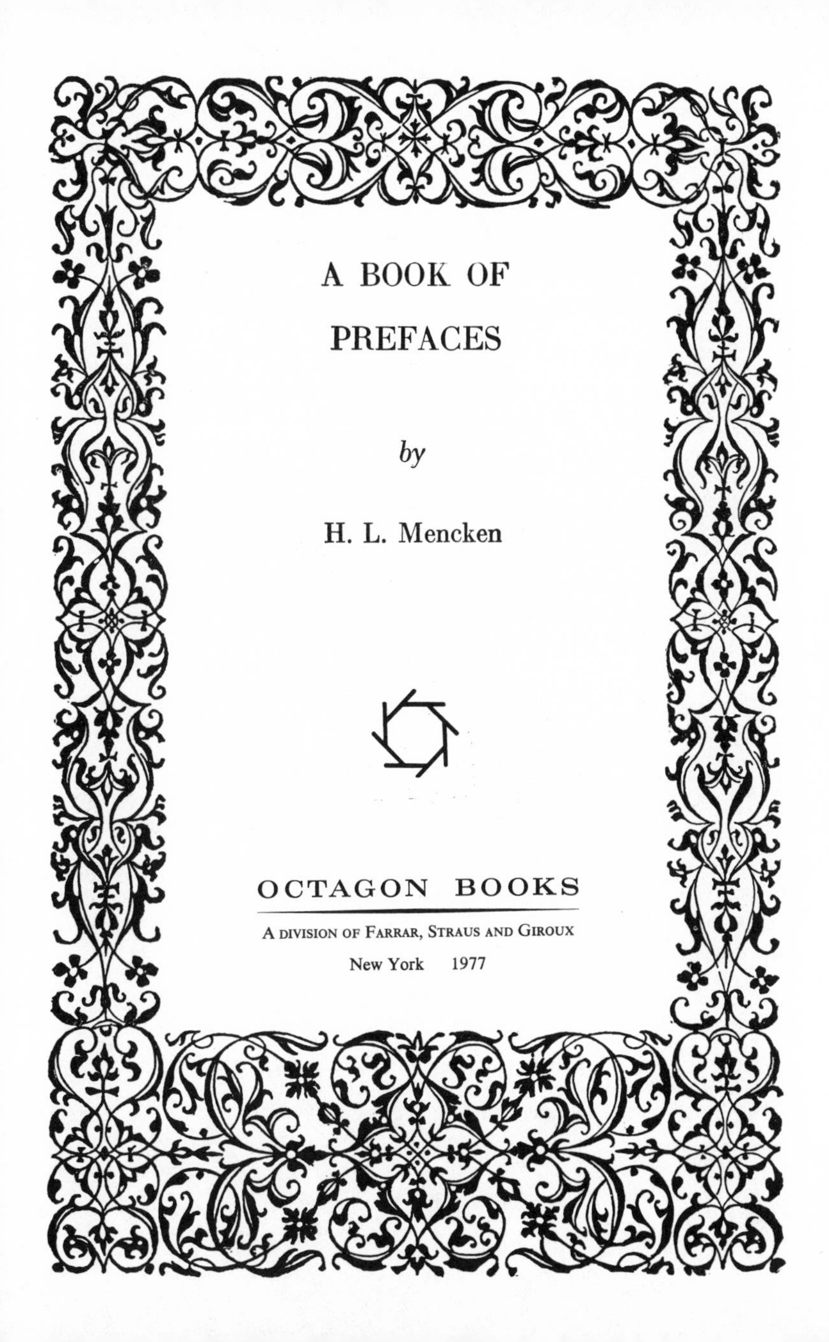

A BOOK OF PREFACES

by

H. L. Mencken

OCTAGON BOOKS

A DIVISION OF FARRAR, STRAUS AND GIROUX

New York 1977

Reprinted 1977
by special arrangement with Alfred A. Knopf, Inc.

OCTAGON BOOKS
A DIVISION OF FARRAR, STRAUS & GIROUX, INC.
19 Union Square West
New York, N.Y. 10003

Library of Congress Cataloging in Publication Data

Mencken, Henry Louis, 1880-1956.
A book of prefaces.

Reprint of the 1928 issue of the ed. published by Knopf, New York.
Includes index.
1. American literature—History and criticism—Addresses, essays, lectures. I. Title.

PS121.M4 1977 810′.9 76-30773
ISBN 0-374-95570-0

Manufactured by Braun-Brumfield, Inc.
Ann Arbor, Michigan
Printed in the United States of America

PREFACE TO THE FIFTH EDITION

Since this book was written, in 1917, all of the men discussed have printed important new works, and one of them, Huneker, has died. From Conrad have come "The Arrow of Gold," "The Rescue" and "The Rover"; from Dreiser, "Free," "Twelve Men," "Hey, Rub-a-Dub-Dub," "A Book About Myself" and "The Color of a Great City"; from Huneker, before his death, "Unicorns," "Bedouins," "Steeplejack" and "Painted Veils," and, since his death, a volume of his letters. All of these books invite discussion, and I have discussed most of them elsewhere. If I were writing the present volume to-day I'd deal with them at some length. But I doubt that the fact would make many changes in the text. What I wrote in 1917 I still believe, in the main, in 1924. So I let "A Book of Prefaces" stand.

H. L. M.

Baltimore, March 15, 1924

CONTENTS

I. JOSEPH CONRAD

A BOOK OF PREFACES

I

JOSEPH CONRAD

§ 1

"UNDER all his stories there ebbs and flows a kind of tempered melancholy, a sense of seeking and not finding . . ." I take the words from a little book on Joseph Conrad by Wilson Follett, privately printed, and now, I believe, out of print.[1] They define both the mood of the stories as works of art and their burden and direction as criticisms of life. Like Dreiser, Conrad is forever fascinated by the "immense indifference of things," the tragic vanity of the blind groping that we call aspiration, the profound meaninglessness of life—fascinated, and left wondering. One looks in vain for an attempt at a solution of

1 Joseph Conrad: A short study of his intellectual and emotional attitude toward his work and of the chief characteristics of his novels, by Wilson Follett; New York, Doubleday, Page & Co. (1915).

the riddle in the whole canon of his work. Dreiser, more than once, seems ready to take refuge behind an indeterminate sort of mysticism, even a facile supernaturalism, but Conrad, from first to last, faces squarely the massive and intolerable fact. His stories are not chronicles of men who conquer fate, nor of men who are unbent and undaunted by fate, but of men who are conquered and undone. Each protagonist is a new Prometheus, with a sardonic ignominy piled upon his helplessness. Each goes down a Greek route to defeat and disaster, leaving nothing behind him save an unanswered question. I can scarcely recall an exception. Kurtz, Lord Jim, Razumov, Nostromo, Captain Whalley, Yanko Goorall, Verloc, Heyst, Gaspar Ruiz, Almayer: one and all they are destroyed and made a mock of by the blind, incomprehensible forces that beset them.

Even in "Youth," "Typhoon," and "The Shadow Line," superficially stories of the indomitable, that same consuming melancholy, that same pressing sense of the irresistible and inexplicable, is always just beneath the surface. Captain Mac Whirr gets the *Nan-Shan* to port at last, but it is a victory that stands quite outside the man himself; he is no more than a marker in the unfathomable game; the elemental forces, fighting one another.

almost disregard him; the view of him that we get is one of disdain, almost one of contempt. So, too, in "Youth." A tale of the spirit's triumph, of youth besting destiny? I do not see it so. To me its significance, like that of "The Shadow Line," is all subjective; it is an aging man's elegy upon the hope and high resolution that the years have blown away, a sentimental reminiscence of what the enigmatical gods have had their jest with, leaving only its gallant memory behind. The whole Conradean system sums itself up in the title of "Victory," an incomparable piece of irony. Imagine a better label for that tragic record of heroic and yet bootless effort, that matchless picture, in microcosm, of the relentlessly cruel revolutions in the macrocosm!

Mr. Follett, perhaps with too much critical facility, finds the cause of Conrad's unyielding pessimism in the circumstances of his own life—his double exile, first from Poland, and then from the sea. But this is surely stretching the facts to fit an hypothesis. Neither exile, it must be plain, was enforced, nor is either irrevocable. Conrad has been back to Poland, and he is free to return to the ships whenever the spirit moves him. I see no reason for looking in such directions for his view of the world, nor even in the direction of his nationality. We detect certain curious qualities in every Slav simply because he is more given than we are to revealing the qualities that are in all of us. Introspection and self-revelation are his habit; he carries the study of man and fate to a point that seems morbid to westerners; he is forever gabbling about what he finds in his own soul. But in the last analysis his verdicts are the immemorial and almost universal ones. Surely his resignationism is not a Slavic copyright; all human philosophies and religions seem doomed to come to it at last. Once it takes shape as the concept of Nirvana, the desire for nothingness, the will to not-will. Again, it is fatalism in this form or that—Mohammedanism, Agnosticism . . . Calvinism! Yet again, it is the "Out, out, brief candle!" of Shakespeare, the "*Eheu fugaces*" of Horace, the "*Vanitas vanitatum; omnia vanitas!*" of the Preacher. Or, to make an end, it is millenarianism, the theory that the world is going to blow up tomorrow, or the day after, or two weeks hence, and that all sweating and striving are thus useless. Search where you will, near or far, in ancient or modern times, and you will never find a first-rate race or an enlightened age, in its moments of highest reflection, that ever gave more than a passing bow to optimism. Even Christian ity, starting out as "glad tidings," has had to take on protective coloration to survive, and today its chief professors moan and blubber like Johann in Herod's rain-barrel. The sanctified are few and far between. The vast majority of us must suffer in hell, just as we suffer on earth. The divine grace, so omnipotent to save, is withheld from us. Why? There, alas, is your insoluble mystery, your riddle of the universe! . . .

This conviction that human life is a seeking without a finding, that its purpose is impenetrable, that joy and sorrow are alike meaningless, you will see written largely in the work of most great creative artists. It is obviously the final message, if any message is genuinely to be found there, of the nine symphonies of Ludwig van Beethoven, or, at any rate, of the three which show any intellectual content at all. Mark Twain, superficially a humourist and hence an optimist, was haunted by it in secret, as Nietzsche was by the idea of eternal recurrence: it forced itself through his guard in "The Mysterious Stranger" and "What is Man?" In Shakespeare, as Shaw has demonstrated, it amounts to a veritable obsession. And what else is there in Balzac, Goethe, Swift, Molière, Turgenev, Ibsen, Dostoyevsky, Romain Rolland, Anatole France? Or in the Zola of "L'Assomoir," "Germinal," "La

Débâcle," the whole Rougon-Macquart series? (The Zola of "Les Quatres Evangiles," and particularly of "Fécondité," turned meliorist and idealist, and became ludicrous.) Or in the Hauptmann of "Fuhrmann Henschel," or in Hardy, or in Sudermann? (I mean, of course, Sudermann the novelist. Sudermann the dramatist is a mere mechanician.) . . . The younger men in all countries, in so far as they challenge the current sentimentality at all, seem to move irresistibly toward the same disdainful skepticism. Consider the last words of "Riders to the Sea." Or Gorky's "Nachtasyl." Or Frank Norris' "McTeague." Or Stephen Crane's "The Blue Hotel." Or the ironical fables of Dunsany. Or Dreiser's "Jennie Gerhardt." Or George Moore's "Sister Teresa."

Conrad, more than any of the other men I have mentioned, grounds his work firmly upon this sense of cosmic implacability, this confession of unintelligibility. The exact point of the story of Kurtz, in "Heart of Darkness," is that it is pointless, that Kurtz's death is as meaningless as his life, that the moral of such a sordid tragedy is a wholesale negation of all morals. And this, no less, is the point of the story of Falk, and of that of Almayer, and of that of Jim. Mr. Follett (he must be a forward-looker in his heart!) finds himself, in the end, unable to accept so profound a determinism unadulterated, and so he injects a gratuitous and mythical romanticism into it, and hymns Conrad "as a comrade, one of a company gathered under the ensign of hope for common war on despair." With even greater error, William Lyon Phelps argues that his books "are based on the axiom of the moral law." [1] The one notion is as unsound as the other. Conrad makes war on nothing; he is pre-eminently *not* a moralist. He swings, indeed, as far from revolt and moralizing as is possible, for he does not even criticize God. His undoubted comradeship, his plain kindliness toward the soul he vivisects, is not the fruit of moral certainty, but of moral agnosticism. He neither protests nor punishes; he merely smiles and pities. Like Mark Twain he might well say: "The more I see of men, the more they amuse me—and the more I pity them." He is *simpatico* precisely because of this ironical commiseration, this infinite disillusionment, this sharp understanding of the narrow limits of human volition and responsibility . . . I have said that he does not criticize God. One may even imagine him pitying God . . .

[1] The Advance of the English Novel. New York, Dodd, Mead & Co., 1916, p. 215.

§ 2

But in this pity, I need not add, there is no touch of sentimentality. No man could be less the romantic, blubbering over the sorrows of his own Werthers. No novelist could have smaller likeness to the brummagem emotion-squeezers of the Kipling type, with their playhouse fustian and their naïve ethical cocksureness. The thing that sets off Conrad from these facile fellows, and from the shallow pseudo-realists who so often coalesce with them and become indistinguishable from them, is precisely his quality of irony, and that irony is no more than a proof of the greater maturity of his personal culture, his essential superiority as a civilized man. It is the old difference between a Huxley and a Gladstone, a philosophy that is profound and a philosophy that is merely comfortable, "*Quid est veritas?*" and "Thus saith the Lord!" He brings into the English fiction of the day, not only an artistry that is vastly more fluent and delicate than the general, but also a highly unusual sophistication, a quite extraordinary detachment from all petty rages and puerile certainties. The winds of doctrine, howling all about him, leave him absolutely unmoved. He belongs to no party and has nothing to teach, save only a mystery as old as man. In the midst of the hysterical splutterings and battle-cries of the Kiplings and Chestertons, the booming pedagogics of the Wellses and Shaws, and the smirking at keyholes of the Bennetts and de Morgans, he stands apart and almost alone, observing the sardonic comedy of man with an eye that sees every point and significance of it, but vouchsafing none of that sophomoric indignation, that Hyde Park wisdom, that flabby moralizing which freight and swamp the modern English novel. "At the centre of his web," says Arthur Symons, "sits an elemental sarcasm discussing human affairs with a calm and cynical ferocity . . . He calls up all the dreams and illusions by which men have been destroyed and saved, and lays them mockingly naked . . . He shows the bare side of every virtue, the hidden heroism of every vice and crime. He summons before him all the injustices that have come to birth out of ignorance and self-love . . . And in all this there is no judgment, only an implacable comprehension, as of one outside nature, to whom joy and sorrow, right and wrong, savagery and civilization, are equal and indifferent . . ."[1]

Obviously, no Englishman! No need to explain

[1] Conrad, in the *Forum,* May, 1915.

(with something akin to apology) that his name is really not Joseph Conrad at all, but Teodor Josef Konrad Karzeniowski, and that he is a Pole of noble lineage, with a vague touch of the Asiatic in him. The Anglo-Saxon mind, in these later days, becomes increasingly incapable of his whole point of view. Put into plain language, his doctrine can only fill it with wonder and fury. That mind is essentially moral in cut; it is believing, certain, indignant; it is as incapable of skepticism, save as a passing coryza of the spirit, as it is of wit, which is skepticism's daughter. Time was when this was not true, as Congreve, Pope, Wycherley and even Thackeray show, but that time was before the Reform Bill of 1832, the great intellectual levelling, the emancipation of the *chandala*. In these our days the Englishman is an incurable foe of distinction, and being so he must needs take in with his mother's milk the delusions which go with that enmity, and particularly the master delusion that all human problems, in the last analysis, are readily soluble, and that all that is required for their solution is to take counsel freely, to listen to wizards, to count votes, to agree upon legislation. This is the prime and immovable doctrine of the *mobile vulgus* set free; it is the loveliest of all the fruits of its defective powers of observation and reasoning, and above all, of its defective knowledge of demonstrated facts, especially in history. Take away this notion that there is some mysterious infallibility in the sense of the majority, this theory that the consensus of opinion is inspired, and the idea of equality begins to wither; in fact, it ceases to have any intelligibility at all. But the notion is not taken away; it is nourished; it flourishes on its own effluvia. And out of it spring the two rules which give direction to all popular thinking, the first being that no concept in politics or conduct is valid (or more accurately respectable), which rises above the comprehension of the great masses of men, or which violates any of their inherent prejudices or superstitions, and the second being that the articulate individual in the mob takes on some of the authority and inspiration of the mob itself, and that he is thus free to set himself up as a soothsayer, so long as he does not venture beyond the aforesaid bounds—in brief, that one man's opinion, provided it observe the current decorum, is as good as any other man's.

Practically, of course, this is simply an invitation to quackery. The man of genuine ideas is hedged in by taboos; the quack finds an audience already agape. The reply to the invitation, in the domain of applied ethics, is the revived and reinforced *Sklavenmoral* that besets all of us of English speech—the huggermugger morality of timorous, whining, unintelligent and unimaginative men—envy turned into law, cowardice sanctified, stupidity made noble, Puritanism. And in the theoretical field there is an even more luxuriant crop of bosh. Mountebanks almost innumerable tell us what we should believe and practice, in politics, religion, philosophy and the arts. England and the United States, between them, house more creeds than all the rest of the world together, and they are more absurd. They rise, they flame, they fall and go out, but always there are new ones, always the latest is worse than the last. What modern civilization save this of ours could have produced Christian Science, or the New Thought, or Billy Sundayism? What other could have yielded up the mawkish bumptiousness of the Uplift? What other could accept gravely the astounding imbecilities of English philanthropy and American law? The native output of fallacy and sentimentality, in fact, is not enough to satisfy the stupendous craving of the mob unleashed; there must needs be a constant importation of the aberrant fancies of other peoples. Let a new messiah leap up with a new message in any part of the world, and at once there is a response from the two great free nations. Once it was Tolstoi with a mouldy asceticism made of catacomb Christianity and senile soul-sickness; again it was Bergson, with a perfumed quasi-philosophy for the boudoirs of the faubourgs; yet again came Rudolf Eucken and Pastor Wagner, with their middle-class beeriness and banality. The list need go no further. It begins with preposterous Indian swamis and yoghis (most of them, to do them justice, diligent Jews from Grand street or the bagnios of Constantinople), and it ends with the fabulous Ibsen of the symbols (no more the real Ibsen than Christ was a prohibitionist), the Ellen Key of the new gyneolatry and the Signorina Montessori of the magical Method. It was a sure instinct that brought Eusapia Palladino to New York. It was the same sure instinct that brought Hall Caine.

I have mentioned Ibsen. A glance at the literature he has spawned in the vulgate is enough to show how much his falser aspects have intrigued the American mind and how little it has reacted to his shining skill as a dramatic craftsman—his one authentic claim upon fame. Read Jennette Lee's "The Ibsen Secret,"[1] perhaps the most successful of all the Ibsen gemaras in English, if you would know the virulence of the national appetite for

[1] New York and London. G. P. Putnam's Sons, 1907.

bogus revelation. And so in all the arts. Whatever is profound and penetrating we stand off from; whatever is facile and shallow, particularly if it reveal a moral or mystical color, we embrace. Ibsen the first-rate dramatist was rejected with indignation precisely because of his merits—his sharp observation, his sardonic realism, his unsentimental logic. But the moment a meretricious and platitudinous ethical purpose began to be read into him—how he protested against it!—he was straightway adopted into our flabby culture. Compare Hauptmann and Brieux, the one a great artist, the other no more than a raucous journalist. Brieux's elaborate proofs that two and two are four have been hailed as epoch-making; one of his worst plays, indeed, has been presented with all the solemn hocus-pocus of a religious rite. But Hauptmann remains almost unknown; even the Nobel Prize did not give him a vogue. Run the roll: Maeterlinck and his languishing supernaturalism, Tagore and his Asiatic wind music, Selma Lagerlöf and her old maid's mooniness, Bernstein, Molnar and company and their out-worn tricks—but I pile up no more names. Consider one fact: the civilization that kissed Maeterlinck on both cheeks, and Tagore perhaps even more intimately, has yet to shake hands with Anatole France. . . .

This bemusement by superficial ideas, this neck-bending to quacks, this endless appetite for sesames and apocalypses, is depressingly visible in our native literature, as it is in our native theology, philosophy and politics. "The British and American mind," says W. L. George,[1] "has been long honeycombed with moral impulse, at any rate since the Reformation; it is very much what the German mind was up to the middle of the Nineteenth Century." The artist, facing an audience which seems incapable of differentiating between æsthetic and ethical values, tends to become a preacher of sonorous nothings, and the actual moralist-propagandist finds his way into art well greased. No other people in Christendom produces so vast a crop of tin-horn haruspices. We have so many Orison Swett Mardens, Martin Tuppers, Edwin Markhams, Gerald Stanley Lees, Dr. Frank Cranes and Dr. Sylvanus Stalls that their output is enough to supply the whole planet. We see, too, constantly, how thin is the barrier separating the chief Anglo-Saxon novelists and playwrights from the pasture of the platitudinarian. Jones and Pinero both made their first strikes, not as the artists they undoubtedly are, but as pinchbeck moralists, moan-

[1] The Intelligence of Woman. Boston, Little, Brown & Co., 1916, p. 6-7.

ing over the sad fact that girls are seduced. Shaw, a highly dexterous dramaturgist, smothers his dramaturgy in a pifflish iconoclasm that is no more than a disguise for Puritanism. Bennett and Wells, competent novelists, turn easily from the novel to the volume of shoddy philosophizing. Kipling, with "Kim" behind him, becomes a vociferous leader-writer of the *Daily Mail* school, whooping a pothouse patriotism, hurling hysterical objurgations at the foe. Even W. L. George, potentially a novelist of sound consideration, drops his craft for the jehad of the suffragettes. Doyle, Barrie, Caine, Locke, Barker, Mrs. Ward, Beresford, Hewlett, Watson, Quiller-Couch—one and all, high and low, they are tempted by the public demand for sophistry, the ready market for pills. A Henry Bordeaux, in France, is an exception; in England he is the rule. The endless thirst to be soothed with cocksure asseverations, the great mob yearning to be dosed and comforted, is the undoing, over there, of three imaginative talents out of five.

And, in America, of nearly five out of five. Winston Churchill may serve as an example. He is a literary workman of very decent skill; the native critics speak of him with invariable respect; his standing within the craft was shown when he was unanimously chosen first president of the Authors' League of America. Examine his books in order. They proceed steadily from studies of human character and destiny, the proper business of the novelist, to mere outpourings of social and economic panaceas, the proper business of leader writers, chautauquas rabble-rousers and hedge politicians. "The Celebrity" and "Richard Carvel," within their limits, are works of art; "The Inside of the Cup" is no more than a compendium of paralogy, as silly and smattering as a speech by William Jennings Bryan or a shocker by Jane Addams. Churchill, with the late Jack London to bear him company, may stand for a large class; in its lower ranks are such men as Reginald Wright Kauffman and Will Levington Comfort. Still more typical of the national taste for moral purpose and quack philosophy are the professional optimists and eye-dimmers, with their two grand divisions, the boarding-school romantics and the Christian Endeavor Society sentimentalists. Of the former I give you George Barr McCutcheon, Owen Wister, the late Richard Harding Davis, and a horde of women—most of them now humanely translated to the moving pictures. Of the latter I give you the fair authors of the "glad" books, so gigantically popular, so lavishly praised in the newspapers—with the wraith of the later Howells, the virtuous, kittenish Howells, floating about in the air above them. No other country can parallel this literature, either in its copiousness or in its banality. It is native and peculiar to a civilization which erects the unshakable certainties of the misinformed and quack-ridden into a national way of life. . . .

§ 3

My business, however, is not with the culture of Anglo-Saxondom, but only with Conrad's place therein. That place is isolated and remote; he is neither of it nor quite in it. In the midst of a futile meliorism which deceives the more, the more it soothes, he stands out like some sinister skeleton at the feast, regarding the festivities with a flickering and impenetrable grin. "To read him," says Arthur Symons, "is to shudder on the edge of a gulf, in a silent darkness." There is no need to be told that he is there almost by accident, that he came in a chance passerby, a bit uncertain of the door. It was not an artistic choice that made him write English instead of French; it was a choice with its roots in considerations far afield. But once made, it concerned him no further. In his first book he was plainly a stranger, and all himself; in his last he is a stranger still—strange in his manner of speech, strange in his view of life, strange, above all, in his glowing and gorgeous artistry, his enthusiasm for beauty *per se,* his absolute detachment from that heresy which would make it no more than a servant to some bald and depressing theory of conduct, some axiom of the uncomprehending. He is, like Dunsany, a pure artist. His work, as he once explained, is not to edify, to console, to improve or to encourage, but simply to get upon paper some shadow of his own eager sense of the wonder and prodigality of life as men live it in the world, and of its unfathomable romance and mystery. "My task," he went on, "is, by the power of the written word, to make you hear, to make you feel—it is, before all, to make you *see.* That—and no more, and it is everything." . . .[1]

This detachment from all infra-and-ultra-artistic purpose, this repudiation of the rôle of propagandist, this avowal of what Nietzsche was fond of calling innocence, explains the failure of Conrad to fit into the pigeon-holes so laboriously prepared for him by critics who must shelve and label or be damned. He is too big for any of

[1] In *The New Review,* Dec., 1897.

them, and of a shape too strange. He stands clear, not only of all the schools and factions that obtain in latter-day English fiction, but also of the whole stream of English literature since the Restoration. He is as isolated a figure as George Moore, and for much the same reason. Both are exotics, and both, in a very real sense, are public enemies, for both war upon the philosophies that caress the herd. Is Conrad the beyond-Kipling, as the early criticism of him sought to make him? Nonsense! As well speak of Mark Twain as the beyond-Petroleum V. Nasby (as, indeed, was actually done). He is not only a finer artist than Kipling; he is a quite different kind of artist. Kipling, within his limits, shows a talent of a very high order. He is a craftsman of the utmost deftness. He gets his effects with almost perfect assurance. Moreover, there is a poet in him; he knows how to reach the emotions. But once his stories are stripped down to the bare carcass their emptiness becomes immediately apparent. The ideas in them are not the ideas of a reflective and perspicacious man, but simply the ideas of a mob-orator, a mouther of inanities, a bugler, a school-girl. Reduce any of them to a simple proposition, and that proposition, in so far as it is intelligible at all, will be ridiculous. It is precisely here that

Conrad leaps immeasurably ahead. His ideas are not only sound; they are acute and unusual. They plough down into the sub-strata of human motive and act. They unearth conditions and considerations that lie concealed from the superficial glance. They get at the primary reactions. In particular and above all, they combat the conception of man as a pet and privy councillor of the gods, working out his own destiny in a sort of vacuum and constantly illumined by infallible revelations of his duty, and expose him as he is in fact: an organism infinitely more sensitive and responsive than other organisms, but still a mere organism in the end, a brother to the wild things and the protozoa, swayed by the same inscrutable fortunes, condemned to the same inchoate errors and irresolutions, and surrounded by the same terror and darkness . . .

But is the Conrad I here describe simply a new variety of moralist, differing from the general only in the drift of the doctrine he preaches? Surely not. He is no more a moralist than an atheist is a theologian. His attitude toward all moral systems and axioms is that of a skeptic who rejects them unanimously, even including, and perhaps especially including, those to which, in moments of æsthetic detachment, he seems to give a formal and resigned sort of assent. It is this constant falling back upon "I do not know," this incessant conversion of the easy logic of romance into the harsh and dismaying logic of fact, that explains his failure to succeed as a popular novelist, despite his skill at evoking emotion, his towering artistic passion, his power to tell a thumping tale. He is talked of, he brings forth a mass of punditic criticism, he becomes in a sense the fashion; but it would be absurd to say that he has made the same profound impression upon the great class of normal novel-readers that Arnold Bennett once made, or H. G. Wells, or William de Morgan in his brief day, or even such cheap-jacks as Anthony Hope Hawkins and William J. Locke. His show fascinates, but his philosophy, in the last analysis, is unbearable. And in particular it is unbearable to women. One rarely meets a woman who, stripped of affection, shows any genuine enthusiasm for a Conrad book, or, indeed, any genuine comprehension of it. The feminine mind, which rules in English fiction, both as producer and as consumer, craves inevitably a more confident and comforting view of the world than Conrad has to offer. It seeks, not disillusion, but illusion. It protects itself against the disquieting questioning of life by pretending that all the riddles have been solved, that each new sage answers them afresh, that a few simple principles suffice to dispose of them. Women, one may say, have to subscribe to absurdities in order to account for themselves at all; it is the instinct of self-preservation which sends them to priests, as to other quacks. This is not because they are unintelligent, but rather because they have that sharp and sure sort of intelligence which is instinctive, and which passes under the name of intuition. It teaches them that the taboos which surround them, however absurd at bottom, nevertheless penalize their courage and curiosity with unescapable dudgeon, and so they become partisans of the existing order, and, per corollary, of the existing ethic. They may be menaced by phantoms, but at all events these phantoms really menace them. A woman who reacted otherwise than with distrust to such a book as "Victory" would be as abnormal as a woman who embraced "Jenseits von Gut und Böse" or "The Inestimable Life of the Great Gargantua."

As for Conrad, he retaliates by approaching the sex somewhat gingerly. His women, in the main, are no more than soiled and tattered cards in a game played by the gods. The effort to erect them into the customary "sympathetic" heroines of fiction always breaks down under the drum fire of the plain facts. He sees quite accurately, it seems to me, how vastly the rôle of women has been exaggerated, how little they amount to in the authentic struggle of man. His heroes are moved by avarice, by ambition, by rebellion, by fear, by that "obscure inner necessity" which passes for nobility or the sense of duty—never by that puerile passion which is the mainspring of all masculine acts and aspirations in popular novels and on the stage. If they yield to amour at all, it is only at the urging of some more powerful and characteristic impulse, *e.g.*, a fantastic notion of chivalry, as in the case of Heyst, or the thirst for dominion, as in the case of Kurtz. The one exception is offered by Razumov—and Razumov is Conrad's picture of a flabby fool, of a sentimentalist destroyed by his sentimentality. Dreiser has shown much the same process in Witla and Cowperwood, but he is less free from the conventional obsession than Conrad; he takes a love affair far more naïvely, and hence far more seriously.

I used to wonder why Conrad never tackled a straight-out story of adultery under Christianity, the standard matter of all our more pretentious fiction and drama. I was curious to see what his ethical agnosticism would make of it. The conclusion I came to at first was that his failure marked the limitations of his courage—in brief, that he hesitated to go against the orthodox axioms and assumptions in the department where they were most powerfully maintained. But it seems to me now that his abstinence has not been the fruit of timidity, but of disdain. He has shied at the hypothesis, not at its implications. His whole work, in truth, is a destructive criticism of the prevailing notion that such a story is momentous and worth telling. The current gyneolatry is as far outside his scheme of things as the current program of rewards and punishments, sins and virtues, causes and effects. He not only sees clearly that the destiny and soul of man are not moulded by petty jousts of sex, as the prophets of romantic love would have us believe; he is so impatient of the fallacy that he puts it as far behind him as possible, and sets his conflicts amid scenes that it cannot penetrate, save as a palpable absurdity. Love, in his stories, is either a feeble phosphorescence or a gigantic grotesquerie. In "Heart of Darkness," perhaps, we get his typical view of it. Over all the frenzy and horror of the tale itself floats the irony of the trusting heart back in Brussels. Here we have his measure of the master sentimentality of them all. . . .

§ 4

As for Conrad the literary craftsman, opposing him for the moment to Conrad the showman of the human comedy, the quality that all who write about him seem chiefly to mark in him is his scorn of conventional form, his tendency to approach his story from two directions at once, his frequent involvement in apparently inextricable snarls of narrative, sub-narrative and sub-sub-narrative. "Lord Jim," for example, starts out in the third person, presently swings into an exhaustive psychological discussion by the mythical Marlow, then goes into a brisk narrative at second (and sometimes at third) hand, and finally comes to a halt upon an unresolved dissonance, a half-heard chord of the ninth: "And that's the end. He passes away under a cloud, inscrutable at heart, forgotten, unforgiven, and excessively romantic." "Falk" is also a story within a story; this time the narrator is "one who had not spoken before, a man over fifty." In "Amy Foster" romance is filtered through the prosaic soul of a country doctor; it is almost as if a statistician told the tale of Horatius at the bridge. In "Under Western Eyes" the obfuscation is achieved by "a teacher of languages," endlessly lamenting his lack of the "high gifts of imagination and expression." In "Youth" and "Heart of Darkness" the chronicler and speculator is the shadowy Marlow, a "cloak to goe inbisabell" for Conrad himself. In "Chance" there are two separate stories, imperfectly welded together. Elsewhere there are hesitations, goings back, interpolations, interludes in the Socratic manner. And almost always there is heaviness in the getting under weigh. In "Heart of Darkness" we are on the twentieth page before we see the mouth of the great river, and in "Falk" we are on the twenty-fourth before we get a glimpse of Falk. "Chance" is nearly half done before the drift of the action is clearly apparent. In "Almayer's Folly" we are thrown into the middle of a story, and do not discover its beginning until we come to "An Outcast of the Islands," a later book. As in structure, so in detail. Conrad pauses to explain, to speculate, to look about. Whole chapters concern themselves with detailed discussions of motives, with exchanges of views, with generalizations abandoned as soon as they are made. Even the author's own story, "A Personal Record" (in the English edition, "Some Reminiscences") starts near the end, and then goes back, halting tortuously, to the beginning.

In the eyes of orthodox criticism, of course, this

is a grave fault. The Kipling-Wells style of swift, shouldering, button-holing writing has accustomed readers and critics alike to a straight course and a rapid tempo. Moreover, it has accustomed them to a forthright certainty and directness of statement; they expect an author to account for his characters at once, and on grounds instantly comprehensible. This omniscience is a part of the prodigality of moral theory that I have been discussing. An author who knows just what is the matter with the world may be quite reasonably expected to know just what is the matter with his hero. Neither sort of assurance, I need not say, is to be found in Conrad. He is an inquirer, not a law-giver; an experimentalist, not a doctor. One constantly derives from his stories the notion that he is as much puzzled by his characters as the reader is—that he, too, is feeling his way among shadowy evidences. The discoveries that we make, about Lord Jim, about Nostromo or about Kurtz, come as fortuitously and as unexpectedly as the discoveries we make about the real figures of our world. The picture is built up bit by bit; it is never flashed suddenly and completely as by best-seller calciums; it remains a bit dim at the end. But in that very dimness, so tantalizing and yet so revealing, lies two-thirds of Conrad's art, or his craft, or his trick, or whatever you choose to call it. What he shows us is blurred at the edges, but so is life itself blurred at the edges. We see least clearly precisely what is nearest to us, and is hence most real to us. A man may profess to understand the President of the United States, but he seldom alleges, even to himself, that he understands his own wife.

In the character and in its reactions, in the act and in the motive: always that tremulousness, that groping, that confession of final bewilderment. "He passes away under a cloud, inscrutable at heart . . ." And the cloud enshrouds the inner man as well as the outer, the secret springs of his being as well as the overt events of his life. "His meanest creatures," says Arthur Symons, "have in them a touch of honour, of honesty, or of heroism; his heroes have always some error, weakness, or mistake, some sin or crime, to redeem." What is Lord Jim, scoundrel and poltroon or gallant knight? What is Captain MacWhirr, hero or simply ass? What is Falk, beast or idealist? One leaves "Heart of Darkness" in that palpitating confusion which is shot through with intense curiosity. Kurtz is at once the most abominable of rogues and the most fantastic of dreamers. It is impossible to differentiate between his vision and his crimes, though all that we look upon as order in the universe stands between them. In Dreiser's novels there is the same anarchy of valuations, and it is chiefly responsible for the rage he excites in the unintelligent. The essential thing about Cowperwood is that he is two diverse beings at once; a puerile chaser of women and a great artist, a guinea pig and half a god. The essential thing about Carrie Meeber is that she remains innocent in the midst of her contaminations, that the virgin lives on in the kept woman. This is not the art of fiction as it is conventionally practised and understood. It is not explanation, labelling, assurance, moralizing. In the cant of newspaper criticism, it does not "satisfy." But the great artist is never one who satisfies in that feeble sense; he leaves the business to mountebanks who do it better. "My purpose," said Ibsen, "is not to answer questions; it is to ask them." The spectator must bring something with him beyond the mere faculty of attention. If, coming to Conrad, he cannot, he is at the wrong door.

§ 5

Conrad's predilection for barbarous scenes and the more bald and shocking sort of drama has an obviously autobiographical basis. His own road ran into strange places in the days of his youth. He moved among men who were menaced by all the terrestrial cruelties, and by the almost unchecked rivalry and rapacity of their fellow men, without any appreciable barriers, whether of law, of convention or of sentimentality, to shield them. The struggle for existence, as he saw it, was well nigh as purely physical among human beings as among the carnivora of the jungle. Some of his stories, and among them his very best, are plainly little more than transcripts of his own experience. He himself is the enchanted boy of "Youth"; he is the ship-master of "Heart of Darkness"; he hovers in the background of all the island books and is visibly present in most of the tales of the sea.

And what he got out of that early experience was more than a mere body of reminiscence; it was a scheme of valuations. He came to his writing years with a sailor's disdain for the trifling hazards and emprises of market places and drawing rooms, and it shows itself whenever he sets pen to paper. A conflict, it would seem, can make no impression upon him save it be colossal. When his men combat, not nature, but other men, they carry over into the business the gigantic method of sailors battling with a tempest. "The Secret

Agent" and "Under Western Eyes" fill the dull back streets of London and Geneva with pursuits, homicides and dynamitings. "Nostromo" is a long record of treacheries, butcheries and carnalities. "A Point of Honor" is coloured by the senseless, insatiable ferocity of Gobineau's "Renaissance." "Victory" ends with a massacre of all the chief personages, a veritable catastrophe of blood. Whenever he turns from the starker lusts to the pale passions of man under civilization, Conrad fails. "The Return" is a thoroughly infirm piece of writing—a second rate magazine story. One concludes at once that the author himself does not believe in it. "The Inheritors" is worse; it becomes, after the first few pages, a flaccid artificiality, a bore. It is impossible to imagine the chief characters of the Conrad gallery in such scenes. Think of Captain MacWhirr reacting to social tradition, Lord Jim immersed in the class war, Lena Hermann seduced by the fashions, Almayer a candidate for office! As well think of Huckleberry Finn at Harvard, or Tom Jones practising law.

These things do not interest Conrad, chiefly, I suppose, because he does not understand them. His concern, one may say, is with the gross anatomy of passion, not with its histology. He seeks to depict emotion, not in its ultimate attenuation, but in its fundamental innocence and fury. Inevitably, his materials are those of what we call melodrama; he is at one, in the bare substance of his tales, with the manufacturers of the baldest shockers. But with a difference!—a difference, to wit, of approach and comprehension, a difference abysmal and revolutionary. He lifts melodrama to the dignity of an important business, and makes it a means to an end that the mere shock-monger never dreams of. In itself, remember, all this up-roar and blood-letting is not incredible, nor even improbable. The world, for all the pressure of order, is still full of savage and stupendous conflicts, of murders and debaucheries, of crimes indescribable and adventures almost unimaginable. One cannot reasonably ask a novelist to deny them or to gloss over them; all one may demand of him is that, if he make artistic use of them, he render them understandable—that he logically account for them, that he give them plausibility by showing their genesis in intelligible motives and colourable events.

The objection to the conventional melodramatist is that he fails to do this. It is not that his efforts are too florid, but that his causes are too puny. For all his exuberance of fancy, he seldom shows us a downright impossible event; what he does constantly show us is an inadequate and hence unconvincing motive. In a cheap theatre we see a bad actor, imperfectly disguised as a viscount, bind a shrieking young woman to the railroad tracks, with an express train approaching. Why does he do it? The melodramatist offers a double-headed reason, the first part being that the viscount is an amalgam of Satan and Don Juan and the second being that the young woman prefers death to dishonour. Both parts are absurd. Our eyes show us at once that the fellow is far more the floorwalker, the head barber, the Knight of Pythias than either the Satan or the Don Juan, and our experience of life tells us that young women in yellow wigs do not actually rate their virginity so dearly. But women are undoubtedly done to death in this way—not every day, perhaps, but now and then. Men bind them, trains run over them, the newspapers discuss the crime, the pursuit of the felon, the ensuing jousting of the jurisconsults. Why, then? The true answer, when it is forthcoming at all, is always much more complex than the melodramatist's answer. It may be so enormously complex, indeed, as to transcend all the normal laws of cause and effect. It may be an answer made up largely, or even wholly, of the fantastic, the astounding, the unearthly reasons of lunacy. That is the chief, if not the only difference between melodrama and reality. The events of the two may be, and often are identical. It is only in their underlying network of causes that they are dissimilar and incommensurate.

Here, in brief, you have the point of essential distinction between the stories of Conrad, a supreme artist in fiction, and the trashy confections of the literary artisans—*e.g.*, Sienkiewicz, Dumas, Lew Wallace, and their kind. Conrad's materials, at bottom, are almost identical with those of the artisans. He, too, has his chariot races, his castaways, his carnivals of blood in the arena. He, too, takes us through shipwrecks, revolutions, assassinations, gaudy heroisms, abominable treacheries. But always he illuminates the nude and amazing event with shafts of light which reveal not only the last detail of its workings, but also the complex of origins and inducements behind it. Always, he throws about it a probability which, in the end, becomes almost inevitability. His "Nostromo," for example, in its externals, is a mere tale of South American turmoil; its materials are those of "Soldiers of Fortune." But what a difference in method, in point of approach, in inner content! Davis was content to show the overt act, scarcely accounting for it at all, and then only in terms of conventional romance. Conrad penetrates to the motive concealed in it, the psychological spring and basis of it, the whole fabric of weakness, habit and aberration underlying it. The one achieved an agreeable romance, and an agreeable romance only. The other achieves an extraordinarily brilliant and incisive study of the Latin-American temperament —a full length exposure of the perverse passions and incomprehensible ideals which provoke presumably sane men to pursue one another like wolves, and of the reactions of that incessant pursuit upon the men themselves, and upon their primary ideas, and upon the institutions under which they live. I do not say that Conrad is always exhaustive in his explanations, or that he is accurate. In the first case I know that he often is not, in the second case I do not know whether he is or he isn't. But I do say that, within the scope of his vision, he is wholly convincing; that the men and women he sets into his scene show ineluctably vivid and persuasive personality; that the theories he brings forward to account for their acts are intelligible; that the effects of those acts, upon actors and immediate spectators alike, are such as might be reasonably expected to issue; that the final impression is one of searching and indubitable veracity. One leaves "Nostromo" with a memory as intense and lucid as that of a real experience. The thing is not mere photography. It is interpretative painting at its highest.

In all his stories you will find this same concern with the inextricable movement of phenomena and noumena between event and event, this same curiosity as to first causes and ultimate effects. Sometimes, as in "The Point of Honor" and "The End of the Tether," he attempts to work out the obscure genesis, in some chance emotion or experience, of an extraordinary series of transactions. At other times, as in "Typhoon," "Youth," "Falk" and "The Shadow Line," his endeavour is to determine the effect of some gigantic and fortuitous event upon the mind and soul of a given man. At yet other times, as in "Almayer's Folly," "Lord Jim" and "Under Western Eyes," it is his aim to show how cause and effect are intricately commingled, so that it is difficult to separate motive from consequence, and consequence from motive. But always it is the process of mind rather than the actual act that interests him. Always he is trying to penetrate the actor's mask and interpret the actor's frenzy. It is this concern with the profounder aspects of human nature, this bold grappling with the deeper and more recondite problems of his art, that gives him consideration as a first-rate artist. He differs from the common novelists of his time as a Beethoven differs from a Mendelssohn. Some of them are quite his equals in technical skill, and a few of them, notably Bennett and Wells, often show an actual superiority, but when it comes to that graver business which underlies all mere virtuosity, he is unmistakably the superior of the whole corps of them.

This superiority is only the more vividly revealed by the shop-worn shoddiness of most of his materials. He takes whatever is nearest to hand, out of his own rich experience or out of the common store of romance. He seems to disdain the petty advantages which go with the invention of novel plots, extravagant characters and unprecedented snarls of circumstance. All the classical doings of anarchists are to be found in "The Secret Agent"; one has heard them copiously credited, of late, to so-called Reds. "Youth," as a story, is no more than an orthodox sea story, and W. Clark Russell contrived better ones. In "Chance" we have a stern father at his immemorial tricks. In "Victory" there are villains worthy of Jack B. Yeats' melodramas of the Spanish Main. In "Nostromo" we encounter the whole stock company of Richard Harding Davis and O. Henry. And in "Under Western Eyes" the protagonist is one who finds his love among the women of his enemies—a situation at the heart of all the military melodramas ever written.

But what Conrad makes of that ancient and fly-blown stuff, that rubbish from the lumber room of the imagination! Consider, for example, "Under Western Eyes," by no means the best of his stories. The plot is that of "Shenandoah" and "Held by the Enemy"—but how brilliantly it is endowed with a new significance, how penetratingly its remotest currents are followed out, how magnificently it is made to fit into that colossal panorama of Holy Russia! It is always this background, this complex of obscure and baffling influences, this drama under the drama, that Conrad spends his skill upon, and not the obvious commerce of the actual stage. It is not the special effect that he seeks, but the general effect. It is not so much man the individual that interests him, as the shadowy accumulation of traditions, instincts and blind chances which shapes the individual's destiny. Here, true enough, we have a full-length portrait of Razumov, glowing with life. But here, far more importantly, we also have an amazingly meticulous and illuminating study of the Russian character, with all its confused mingling of Western realism and Oriental fogginess, its crazy tendency to go shooting off into the spaces of an incomprehensible metaphysic, its general transcendence of all that we Celts and Saxons and Latins hold to be true of human motive and human act. Russia is a world apart: that is the sum and substance of the tale. In the island stories we have the same elaborate projection of the East, of its fantastic barbarism, of brooding Asia. And in the sea stories we have, perhaps for the first time in English fiction, a vast and adequate picture of the sea, the symbol at once of man's eternal striving and of his eternal impotence. Here, at last, the colossus has found its interpreter. There is in "Typhoon" and "The Nigger of the Narcissus," and, above all, in "The Mirror of the Sea," a poetic evocation of the sea's stupendous majesty that is unparalleled outside the ancient sagas. Conrad describes it with a degree of graphic skill that is superb and incomparable. He challenges at once the pictorial vigour of Hugo and the aesthetic sensitiveness of Lafcadio Hearn, and surpasses them both. And beyond this mere dazzling visualization, he gets into his pictures an overwhelming sense of that vast drama of which they are no more than the flat, lifeless representation —of that inexorable and uncompassionate struggle which is life itself. The sea to him is a living thing, an omnipotent and unfathomable thing, almost a god. He sees it as the Eternal Enemy, deceitful in its caresses, sudden in its rages, relentless in its enmities, and forever a mystery.

§ 6

Conrad's first novel, "Almayer's Folly," was printed in 1895. He tells us in "A Personal Record" that it took him seven years to write it—seven years of pertinacious effort, of trial and error, of learning how to write. He was, at this time thirty-eight years old. Seventeen years before, landing in England to fit himself for the British merchant service, he had made his first acquaintance with the English language. The interval had been spent almost continuously at sea—in the Eastern islands, along the China coast, on the Congo and in the South Atlantic. That he hesitated between French and English is a story often told, but he himself is authority for the statement that it is more symbolical than true. Flaubert, in those days, was his idol, as we know, but the speech of his daily business won, and English literature reaped the greatest of all its usufructs from English sea power. To this day there are marks of his origins in his style. His periods, more than once, have an inept and foreign smack. In fishing for the right phrase one sometimes feels that he finds a

French phrase, or even a Polish phrase, and that it loses something by being done into English.

The credit for discovering "Almayer's Folly," as the publishers say, belongs to Edward Garnett, then a reader for T. Fisher Unwin. The book was brought out modestly and seems to have received little attention. The first edition, it would appear, ran to no more than a thousand copies; at all events, specimens of it are now very hard to find, and collectors pay high prices for them. When "An Outcast of the Islands" followed, a year later, a few alert readers began to take notice of the author, and one of them was Sir (then Mr.) Hugh Clifford, a former Governor of the Federated Malay States and himself the author of several excellent books upon the Malay. Clifford gave Conrad encouragement privately and talked him up in literary circles, but the majority of English critics remained unaware of him. After an interval of two years, during which he struggled between his desire to write and the temptation to return to the sea, he published "The Nigger of the Narcissus."[1] It made a fair success of esteem, but still there was no recognition of the author's true stature. Then followed "Tales of Unrest" and "Lord Jim," and

[1] Printed in the United States as Children of the Sea, but now restored to its original title.

after them the feeblest of all the Conrad books, "The Inheritors," written in collaboration with Ford Madox Hueffer. It is easy to see in this collaboration, and no less in the character of the book, an indication of irresolution, and perhaps even of downright loss of hope. But success, in fact, was just around the corner. In 1902 came "Youth," and straightway Conrad was the lion of literary London. The chorus of approval that greeted it was almost a roar; all sorts of critics and reviewers, from H. G. Wells to W. L. Courtney, and from John Galsworthy to W. Robertson Nicoll, took a hand. Writing home to the New York *Times*, W. L. Alden reported that he had "not heard one dissenting voice in regard to the book," but that the praise it received "was unanimous," and that the newspapers and literary weeklies rivalled one another "in their efforts to express their admiration for it."

This benign whooping, however, failed to awaken the enthusiasm of the mass of novel-readers and brought but meagre orders from the circulating libraries. "Typhoon" came upon the heels of "Youth," but still the sales of the Conrad books continued small and the author remained in very uncomfortable circumstances. Even after four or five years he was still so poor that he was glad to accept a modest pension from the British Civil List. This official recognition of his genius, when it came at last, seems to have impressed the public, characteristically enough, far more than his books themselves had done, and the foundations were thus laid for that wider recognition of his genius which now prevails. But getting him on his legs was slow work, and such friends as Hueffer, Clifford and Galsworthy had to do a lot of arduous log-rolling. Even after the splash made by "Youth" his publishing arrangements seem to have remained somewhat insecure. His first eleven books show six different imprints; it was not until his twelfth that he settled down to a publisher. His American editions tell an even stranger story. The first six of them were brought out by six different publishers; the first eight by no less than seven. But to-day he has a regular American publisher at last, and in England a complete edition of his works is in progress.

Thanks to the indefatigable efforts of that American publisher (who labours for Gene Stratton-Porter and Gerald Stanley Lee in the same manner) Conrad has been forced upon the public notice in the United States, and it is the fashion among all who pretend to aesthetic consciousness to read him, or, at all events, to talk about him. His books have been brought together in a uniform edition for the newly intellectual, bound in blue leather, like the "complete library sets" of Kipling, O. Henry, Guy de Maupassant and Paul de Kock. The more literary newspapers print his praises; he is hymned by professorial critics as a prophet of virtue; his genius is certificated by such diverse authorities as Hildegarde Hawthorne and Louis Joseph Vance; I myself lately sat on a Conrad Committee, along with Booth Tarkington, David Belasco, Irvin Cobb, Walter Pritchard Eaton and Hamlin Garland—surely an astounding posse of *literati!* Moreover, Conrad himself shows a disposition to reach out for a wider audience. His "Victory," first published in *Munsey's Magazine*, revealed obvious efforts to be intelligible to the general. A few more turns of the screw and it might have gone into the *Saturday Evening Post*, between serials by Harris Dickson and Rex Beach.

Meanwhile, in the shadow of this painfully growing celebrity as a novelist, Conrad takes on conderation as a bibelot, and the dealers in first editions probably make more profit out of some of his books than ever he has made himself. His manuscripts are cornered, I believe, by an eminent collector of literary curiosities in New York, who seems to have a contract with the novelist to take them as fast as they are produced—perhaps the only arrangement of the sort in literary history. His first editions begin to bring higher premiums than those of any other living author. Considering the fact that the oldest of them is less than twenty-five years old, they probably set new records for the trade. Even the latest in date are eagerly sought, and it is not uncommon to see an English edition of a Conrad book sold at an advance in New York within a month of its publication.[1]

As I hint, however, there is not much reason to believe that this somewhat extravagant fashion is based upon any genuine liking, or any very wide-

[1] Here are some actual prices from booksellers' catalogues:

	1914	1916	1920
Almayer's Folly (1895)	$12.	$24.	$40.
An Outcast of the Islands (1896)	11.50	20.	35.
The Nigger of the Narcissus (1898)	7.50	20.	35.
Tales of Unrest (1898)	12.50	20.	35.
Lord Jim (1900)	7.50	22.50	25.
The Inheritors (1901)	12.	20.	30.
Youth (1902)	5.	7.50	25.
Typhoon (1903)	4.	5.50	16.
Romance (1903)	5.	7.50	9.
Nostromo (1904)	2.50	4.50	7.50
The Mirror of the Sea (1906)	5.	11.	15.
A Set of Six (1908)	3.	7.50	10.
Under Western Eyes (1911)	4.50	4.50	6.
Some Reminiscences (1912)	4.50	9.	15.
Chance (1913)	2.	5.	15.
Victory (1915)	2.	2.50	4.25

spread understanding. The truth is that, for all the adept tub-thumping of publishers, Conrad's sales still fall a good deal behind those of even the most modest of best-seller manufacturers, and that the respect with which his successive volumes are received is accompanied by enthusiasm in a relatively narrow circle only. A clan of Conrad fanatics exists, and surrounding it there is a body of readers who read him because it is the intellectual thing to do, and who talk of him because talking of him is expected. But beyond that he seems to make little impression. When "Victory" was printed in *Munsey's Magazine* it was a failure; no other single novel, indeed, contributed more toward the abandonment of the policy of printing a complete novel in each issue. The other popular magazines show but small inclination for Conrad manuscripts. Some time ago his account of a visit to Poland in war-time was offered on the American market by an English author's agent. At the start a price of $2,500 was put upon it, but after vainly inviting buyers for a couple of months it was finally disposed of to a literary newspaper which seldom spends so much as $2,500, I daresay, for a whole month's supply of copy.

In the United States, at least, novelists are made and unmade, not by critical majorities, but by women, male and female. The art of fiction among us, as Henry James once said, "is almost exclusively feminine." In the books of such a man as William Dean Howells it is difficult to find a single line that is typically and exclusively masculine. One could easily imagine Edith Wharton, or Mrs. Watts, or even Agnes Repplier, writing all of them. When a first-rate novelist emerges from obscurity it is almost always by some fortuitous plucking of the dexter string. "Sister Carrie," for example, has made a belated commercial success, not because its dignity as a human document is understood, but because it is mistaken for a sad tale of amour, not unrelated to "The Woman Thou Gavest Me" and "Dora Thorne." In Conrad there is no such sweet bait for the fair and sentimental. The sedentary multipara, curled up in her boudoir on a rainy afternoon, finds nothing to her taste in his grim tales. The Conrad philosophy is harsh, unyielding, repellent. The Conrad heroes are nearly all boors and ruffians. Their very love-making has something sinister and abhorrent in it; one cannot imagine them in the moving pictures, played by tailored beauties with long eye-lashes. More, I venture that the censors would object to them, even disguised as floor-walkers. Surely that would be a besotted board which would pass the irregular amours of Lord Jim, the domestic brawls of Almayer, the revolting devil's mass of Kurtz, Falk's disgusting feeding in the Southern Ocean, or the butchery on Heyst's island. Stevenson's "Treasure Island" has been put upon the stage, but "An Outcast of the Islands" would be as impossible there as "Barry Lyndon" or "La Terre." The world fails to breed actors for such rôles, or stage managers to penetrate such travails of the spirit, or audiences for the revelation thereof.

With the Conrad cult, so discreetly nurtured out of a Barabbasian silo, there arises a considerable Conrad literature, most of it quite valueless. Huneker's essay, in "Ivory, Apes and Peacocks," [1] gets little beyond the obvious; William Lyon Phelps, in "The Advance of the English Novel," achieves only a meagre judgment; [2] Frederic Taber Cooper tries to estimate such things as "The Secret Agent" and "Under Western Eyes" in terms of the Harvard enlightenment; [3] John Galsworthy wastes himself upon futile comparisons; [4] even Sir Hugh Clifford, for all his quick insight, makes irrelevant objections to Conrad's principles of Malay

[1] New York, Chas. Scribner's Sons, 1915, pp. 1-21.

[2] New York, Dodd, Mead & Co., 1916, pp. 192-217.

[3] Some English Story Tellers: A Book of the Younger Novelists; New York, Henry Holt & Co., 1912, pp. 1-30.

[4] A Disquisition on Conrad, *Fortnightly Review*, April, 1908.

psychology.[1] Who cares? Conrad is his own God, and creates his own Malay! The best of the existing studies of Conrad, despite certain sentimentalities arising out of youth and schooling, is in the book of Wilson Follett, before mentioned. The worst is in the official biography by Richard Curle,[2] for which Conrad himself obtained a publisher and upon which his *imprimatur* may be thus assumed to lie. If it does, then its absurdities are nothing new, for we all know what a botch Ibsen made of accounting for himself. But, even so, the assumption stretches the probabilities more than once. Surely it is hard to think of Conrad putting "Lord Jim" below "Chance" and "The Secret Agent" on the ground that it "raises a fierce moral issue." Nothing, indeed, could be worse nonsense —save it be an American critic's doctrine that "Conrad denounces pessimism." "Lord Jim" no more raises a moral issue than "The Titan." It is, if anything, a devastating exposure of a moral issue. Its villain is almost heroic; its hero, judged by his peers, is a scoundrel. . . .

Hugh Walpole, himself a competent novelist, does

[1] The Genius of Mr. Joseph Conrad, *North American Review*, June, 1904.

[2] Joseph Conrad: A Study; New York, Doubleday, Page & Co., 1914.

far better in his little volume, "Joseph Conrad." [1] In its brief space he is unable to examine all of the books in detail, but he at least manages to get through a careful study of Conrad's method, and his professional skill and interest make it valuable.

§ 7

There is a notion that judgments of living artists are impossible. They are bound to be corrupted, we are told, by prejudice, false perspective, mob emotion, error. The question whether this or that man is great or small is one which only posterity can answer. A silly begging of the question, for doesn't posterity also make mistakes? Shakespeare's ghost has seen two or three posterities, beautifully at odds. Even today, it must notice a difference in flitting from London to Berlin. The shade of Milton has been tricked in the same way. So, also, has Johann Sebastian Bach's. It needed a Mendelssohn to rescue it from Coventry—and now Mendelssohn himself, once so shining a light, is condemned to the shadows in his turn. We are not dead yet; we are here, and it is now. Therefore, let us at least venture, guess, opine.

My own conviction, sweeping all those reaches of

[1] Joseph Conrad; London, Nisbet & Co. (1916).

living fiction that I know, is that Conrad's figure stands out from the field like the Alps from the Piedmont plain. He not only has no masters in the novel; he has scarcely a colourable peer. Perhaps Thomas Hardy and Anatole France—old men both, their work behind them. But who else? James is dead. Meredith is dead. So is George Moore, though he lingers on. So are all the Russians of the first rank; Andrieff, Gorki and their like are light cavalry. In Sudermann, Germany has a writer of short stories of very high calibre, but where is the German novelist to match Conrad? Clara Viebig? Thomas Mann? Gustav Frenssen? Arthur Schnitzler? Surely not! As for the Italians, they are either absurd tear-squeezers or more absurd harlequins. As for the Spaniards and the Scandinavians, they would pass for geniuses only in Suburbia. In America, setting aside an odd volume here and there, one can discern only Dreiser—and of Dreiser's limitations I shall discourse anon. There remains England. England has the best second-raters in the world; nowhere else is the general level of novel writing so high; nowhere else is there a corps of journeyman novelists comparable to Wells, Bennett, Benson, Walpole, Beresford, George, Galsworthy, Hichens, De Morgan, Miss Sinclair, Hewlett and company. They have a prodigious facility; they know how to write; even the least of them is, at all events, a more competent artisan than, say, Dickens, or Bulwer-Lytton, or Sienkiewicz, or Zola. But the literary *grande passion* is simply not in them. They get nowhere with their suave and interminable volumes. Their view of the world and its wonders is narrow and superficial. They are, at bottom, no more than clever mechanicians.

As Galsworthy has said, Conrad lifts himself immeasurably above them all. One might well call him, if the term had not been cheapened into cant, a cosmic artist. His mind works upon a colossal scale; he conjures up the general out of the particular. What he sees and describes in his books is not merely this man's aspiration or that woman's destiny, but the overwhelming sweep and devastation of universal forces, the great central drama that is at the heart of all other dramas, the tragic struggles of the soul of man under the gross stupidity and obscene joking of the gods. "In the novels of Conrad," says Galsworthy, "nature is first, man is second." But not a mute, a docile second! He may think, as Walpole argues, that "life is too strong, too clever and too remorseless for the sons of men," but he does not think that they are too weak and poor in spirit to challenge it. It is the challenging that engrosses him, and enchants him, and raises up the magic of his wonder. It is as futile, in the end, as Hamlet's or Faust's—but still a gallant and a gorgeous adventure, a game uproariously worth the playing, an enterprise "inscrutable . . . and excessively romantic." . . .

If you want to get his measure, read "Youth" or "Falk" or "Heart of Darkness," and then try to read the best of Kipling. I think you will come to some understanding, by that simple experiment, of the difference between an adroit artisan's bag of tricks and the lofty sincerity and passion of a first-rate artist.

II. THEODORE DREISER

II

THEODORE DREISER

§ 1

OUT of the desert of American fictioneering, so populous and yet so dreary, Dreiser stands up—a phenomenon unescapably visible, but disconcertingly hard to explain. What forces combined to produce him in the first place, and how has he managed to hold out so long against the prevailing blasts—of disheartening misunderstanding and misrepresentation, of Puritan suspicion and opposition, of artistic isolation, of commercial seduction? There is something downright heroic in the way the man has held his narrow and perilous ground, disdaining all compromise, unmoved by the cheap success that lies so inviting around the corner. He has faced, in his day, almost every form of attack that a serious artist can conceivably encounter, and yet all of them together have scarcely budged him an inch. He still plods along in the laborious, cheerless way he first marked out for himself; he is quite as undaunted by baited praise as by bludgeoning, malignant abuse; his later novels are, if anything, more unyieldingly dreiserian than his earliest. As one who has long sought to entice him in this direction or that, fatuously presuming to instruct him in what would improve him and profit him, I may well bear a reluctant and resigned sort of testimony to his gigantic steadfastness. It is almost as if any change in his manner, any concession to what is usual and esteemed, any amelioration of his blind, relentless exercises of *force majeure,* were a physical impossibility. One feels him at last to be authentically no more than a helpless instrument (or victim) of that inchoate flow of forces which he himself is so fond of depicting as at once the answer to the riddle of life, and a riddle ten times more vexing and accursed.

And his origins, as I say, are quite as mysterious as his motive power. To fit him into the unrolling chart of American, or even of English fiction is extremely difficult. Save one thinks of H. B. Fuller (whose "With the Procession" and "The Cliff-Dwellers" are still remembered by Huneker, but by whom else? [1]), he seems to have had no fore-runner

[1] Fuller's comparative obscurity is one of the strangest phenomena of American letters. Despite his high achievement, he is seldom discussed, or even mentioned. Back in 1899 he was already so far forgotten that William Archer mistook his name, calling him Henry Y. Puller. *Vide* Archer's pamphlet, The American Language; New York, 1899.

among us, and for all the discussion of him that goes on, he has few avowed disciples, and none of them gets within miles of him. One catches echoes of him, perhaps, in Willa Sibert Cather, in Mary S. Watts, in David Graham Phillips, in Sherwood Anderson and in Joseph Medill Patterson, but, after all, they are no more than echoes. In Robert Herrick the thing descends to a feeble parody; in imitators further removed to sheer burlesque. All the latter-day American novelists of consideration are vastly more facile than Dreiser in their philosophy, as they are in their style. In the fact, perhaps, lies the measure of their difference. What they lack, great and small, is the gesture of pity, the note of awe, the profound sense of wonder—in a phrase, that "soberness of mind" which William Lyon Phelps sees as the hallmark of Conrad and Hardy, and which even the most stupid cannot escape in Dreiser. The normal American novel, even in its most serious forms, takes colour from the national cocksureness and superficiality. It runs monotonously to ready explanations, a somewhat infantile smugness and hopefulness, a habit of reducing the unknowable to terms of the not worth knowing. What it cannot explain away with ready formulae, as in the later Winston Churchill, it snickers over as scarcely worth explaining at all, as in the later

Howells. Such a brave and tragic book as "Ethan Frome" is so rare as to be almost singular, even with Mrs. Wharton. There is, I daresay, not much market for that sort of thing. In the arts, as in the concerns of everyday, the American seeks escape from the insoluble by pretending that it is solved. A comfortable phrase is what he craves beyond all things—and comfortable phrases are surely not to be sought in Dreiser's stock.

I have heard argument that he is a follower of Frank Norris, and two or three facts lend it a specious probability. "McTeague" was printed in 1899; "Sister Carrie" a year later. Moreover, Norris was the first to see the merit of the latter book, and he fought a gallant fight, as literary advisor to Doubleday, Page & Co., against its suppression after it was in type. But this theory runs aground upon two circumstances, the first being that Dreiser did not actually read "McTeague," nor, indeed, grow aware of Norris, until after "Sister Carrie" was completed, and the other being that his development, once he began to write other books, was along paths far distant from those pursued by Norris himself. Dreiser, in truth, was a bigger man than Norris from the start; it is to the latter's unending honour that he recognized the fact instanter, and yet did all he could to help his rival.

It is imaginable, of course, that Norris, living fifteen years longer, might have overtaken Dreiser, and even surpassed him; one finds an arrow pointing that way in "Vandover and the Brute" (not printed until 1914). But it swings sharply around in "The Epic of the Wheat." In the second volume of that incomplete trilogy, "The Pit," there is an obvious concession to the popular taste in romance; the thing is so frankly written down, indeed, that a play has been made of it, and Broadway has applauded it. And in "The Octopus," despite some excellent writing, there is a descent to a mysticism so fantastic and preposterous that it quickly passes beyond serious consideration. Norris, in his day, swung even lower—for example, in "A Man's Woman" and in some of his short stories. He was a pioneer, perhaps only half sure of the way he wanted to go, and the evil lures of popular success lay all about him. It is no wonder that he sometimes seemed to lose his direction.

Émile Zola is another literary father whose paternity grows dubious on examination. I once printed an article exposing what seemed to me to be a Zolaesque attitude of mind, and even some trace of the actual Zola manner, in "Jennie Gerhardt"; there came from Dreiser the news that he had never read a line of Zola, and knew nothing about his novels. Not a complete answer, of course; the influence might have been exerted at second hand. But through whom? I confess that I am unable to name a likely medium. The effects of Zola upon Anglo-Saxon fiction have been almost *nil;* his only avowed disciple, George Moore, has long since recanted and reformed; he has scarcely rippled the prevailing romanticism. . . . Thomas Hardy? Here, I daresay, we strike a better scent. There are many obvious likenesses between "Tess of the D'Urbervilles" and "Jennie Gerhardt" and again between "Jude the Obscure" and "Sister Carrie." All four stories deal penetratingly and poignantly with the essential tragedy of women; all disdain the petty, specious explanations of popular fiction; in each one finds a poetical and melancholy beauty. Moreover, Dreiser himself confesses to an enchanted discovery of Hardy in 1896, three years before "Sister Carrie" was begun. But it is easy to push such a fact too hard, and to search for likenesses and parallels that are really not there. The truth is that Dreiser's points of contact with Hardy might be easily matched by many striking points of difference, and that the fundamental ideas in their novels, despite a common sympathy, are anything but identical. Nor does one apprehend any ponderable result of Dreiser's youthful enthusiasm for

Balzac, which antedated his discovery of Hardy by two years. He got from both men a sense of the scope and dignity of the novel; they taught him that a story might be a good one, and yet considerably more than a story; they showed him the essential drama of the commonplace. But that they had more influence in forming his point of view, or even in shaping his technique, than any one of half a dozen other gods of those young days—this I scarcely find. In the structure of his novels, and in their manner of approach to life no less, they call up the work of Dostoyevsky and Turgenev far more than the work of either of these men—but of all the Russians save Tolstoi (as of Flaubert) Dreiser himself tells us that he was ignorant until ten years after "Sister Carrie." In his days of preparation, indeed, his reading was so copious and so disorderly that antagonistic influences must have well-nigh neutralized one another, and so left the curious youngster to work out his own method and his own philosophy. Stevenson went down with Balzac, Poe with Hardy, Dumas *fils* with Tolstoi. There were even months of delight in Sienkiewicz, Lew Wallace and E. P. Roe! The whole repertory of the pedagogues had been fought through in school and college: Dickens, Thackeray, Hawthorne, Washington Irving, Kingsley, Scott. Only

Irving and Hawthorne seem to have made deep impressions. "I used to lie under a tree," says Dreiser, "and read 'Twice Told Tales' by the hour. I thought 'The Alhambra' was a perfect creation, and I still have a lingering affection for it." Add Bret Harte, George Ebers, William Dean Howells, Oliver Wendell Holmes, and you have a literary stew indeed! . . . But for all its bubbling I see a far more potent influence in the chance discovery of Spencer and Huxley at twenty-three—the year of choosing! Who, indeed, will ever measure the effect of those two giants upon the young men of that era—Spencer with his inordinate meticulousness, his relentless pursuit of facts, his overpowering syllogisms, and Huxley with his devastating agnosticism, his insatiable questionings of the old axioms, above all, his brilliant style? Huxley, it would appear, has been condemned to the scientific hulks, along with bores innumerable and unspeakable; one looks in vain for any appreciation of him in treatises on beautiful letters.[1] And yet the man was a

[1] For example, in The Cambridge History of English Literature, which runs to fourteen large volumes and a total of nearly 10,000 pages, Huxley receives but a page and a quarter of notice, and his remarkable mastery of English is barely mentioned in passing. His two debates with Gladstone, in which he did some of the best writing of the century, are not noticed at all.

superb artist in works, a master-writer even more than a master-biologist, one of the few truly great stylists that England has produced since the time of Anne. One can easily imagine the effect of two such vigorous and intriguing minds upon a youth groping about for self-understanding and self-expression. They swept him clean, he tells us, of the lingering faith of his boyhood—a mediaeval, Rhenish Catholicism;—more, they filled him with a new and eager curiosity, an intense interest in the life that lay about him, a desire to seek out its hidden workings and underlying causes. A young man set afire by Huxley might perhaps make a very bad novelist, but it is a certainty that he could never make a sentimental and superficial one. There is no need to go further than this single moving adventure to find the genesis of Dreiser's disdain of the current platitudes, his sense of life as a complex biological phenomenon, only dimly comprehended, and his tenacious way of thinking things out, and of holding to what he finds good. Ah, that he had learned from Huxley, not only how to inquire, but also how to report! That he had picked up a talent for that dazzling style, so sweet to the ear, so damnably persuasive, so crystal-clear!

But the more one examines Dreiser, either as writer or as theorist of man, the more his essential isolation becomes apparent. He got a habit of mind from Huxley, but he completely missed Huxley's habit of writing. He got a view of woman from Hardy, but he soon changed it out of all resemblance. He got a certain fine ambition and gusto out of Balzac, but all that was French and characteristic he left behind. So with Zola, Howells, Tolstoi and the rest. The tracing of likenesses quickly becomes rabbinism, almost cabalism. The differences are huge and sprout up in all directions. Nor do I see anything save a flaming up of colonial passion in the current efforts to fit him into a German frame, and make him an agent of Prussian frightfulness in letters. Such childish gabble one looks for in the New York *Times*, and there is where one actually finds it. Even the literary monthlies have stood clear of it; it is important only as material for that treatise upon the patrioteer and his bawling which remains to be written. The name of the man, true enough, is obviously Germanic, and he has told us himself, in "A Traveler at Forty," how he sought out and found the tombs of his ancestors in some little town of the Rhine country. There are more of these genealogical revelations in "A Hoosier Holiday," but they show a Rhenish strain that was already running thin in boyhood. No one, indeed, who reads a Dreiser novel can fail to see the gap separating the author from these half-forgotten forbears. He shows even less of German influence than of English influence.

There is, as a matter of fact, little in modern German fiction that is intelligibly comparable to "Jennie Gerhardt" and "The Titan," either as a study of man or as a work of art. The naturalistic movement of the eighties was launched by men whose eyes were upon the theatre, and it is in that field that nine-tenths of its force has been spent. "German naturalism," says George Madison Priest, quoting Gotthold Klee's "Grunzüge der deutschen Literaturgeschichte" "created a new type only in the drama." [1] True enough, it has also produced occasional novels, and some of them are respectable. Gustav Frenssen's "Jörn Uhl" is a specimen: it has been done into English. Another is Clara Viebig's "Das tägliche Brot," which Ludwig Lewisohn compares to George Moore's "Esther Waters." Yet another is Thomas Mann's "Buddenbrooks." But it would be absurd to cite these works as evidences of a national quality, and doubly absurd to think of them as inspiring such books as "Jennie Gerhardt" and "The Titan," which excel them in every-

[1] A Brief History of German Literature; New York, Chas. Scribner's Sons, 1909.

thing save workmanship. The case of Mann reveals a tendency that is visible in nearly all of his contemporaries. Starting out as an agnostic realist not unlike the Arnold Bennett of "The Old Wives' Tale," he has gradually taken on a hesitating sort of romanticism, and in one of his later books, "Königliche Hoheit" (in English, "Royal Highness") he ends upon a note of sentimentalism borrowed from Wagner's "Ring." Fräulein Viebig has also succumbed to banal and extra-artistic purposes. Her "Die Wacht am Rhein," for all its merits in detail, is, at bottom, no more than an eloquent hymn to patriotism—a theme which almost always baffles novelists. As for Frenssen, he is a parson by trade, and carries over into the novel a good deal of the windy moralizing of the pulpit. All of these German naturalists—and they are the only German novelists worth considering—share the weakness of Zola, their *Stammvater*. They, too, fall into the morass that engulfed "Fécondité," and make sentimental propaganda.

I go into this matter in detail, not because it is intrinsically of any moment, but because the effort to depict Dreiser as a secret agent of the Wilhelmstrasse, told off to inject subtle doses of *Kultur* into a naïve and pious people, has taken on the proportions of an organized movement. The same critical imbecility which detects naught save a Tom cat in Frank Cowperwood can find naught save an abhorrent foreigner in Cowperwood's creator. The truth is that the trembling patriots of letters, male and female, are simply at their old game of seeing a man under the bed. Dreiser, in fact, is densely ignorant of German literature, as he is of the better part of French literature, and of much of English literature. He did not even read Hauptmann until after "Jennie Gerhardt" had been written, and such typical German moderns as Ludwig Thoma, Otto Julius Bierbaum and Richard Dehmel remain as strange to him as Heliogabalus.

§ 2

In his manner, as opposed to his matter, he is more the Teuton, for he shows all of the racial patience and pertinacity and all of the racial lack of humour. Writing a novel is as solemn a business to him as trimming a beard is to a German barber. He blasts his way through his interminable stories by something not unlike main strength; his writing, one feels, often takes on the character of an actual siege operation, with tunnellings, drum fire, assaults in close order and hand-to-hand fighting. Once, seeking an analogy, I called him the

Hindenburg of the novel. If it holds, then "The 'Genius'" is his Poland. The field of action bears the aspect, at the end, of a hostile province meticulously brought under the yoke, with every road and lane explored to its beginning, and every crossroads village laboriously taken, inventoried and policed. Here is the very negation of Gallic lightness and intuition, and of all other forms of impressionism as well. Here is no series of illuminating flashes, but a gradual bathing of the whole scene with white light, so that every detail stands out.

And many of those details, of course, are trivial; even irritating. They do not help the picture; they muddle and obscure it; one wonders impatiently what their meaning is, and what the purpose may be of revealing them with such a precise, portentous air. . . . Turn to page 703 of "The 'Genius.'" By the time one gets there, one has hewn and hacked one's way through 702 large pages of fine print —97 long chapters, more than 250,000 words. And yet, at this hurried and impatient point, with the *coda* already begun, Dreiser halts the whole narrative to explain the origin, nature and inner meaning of Christian Science, and to make us privy to a lot of chatty stuff about Mrs. Althea Jones, a professional healer, and to supply us with detailed plans and specifications of the apartment house in which she lives, works her tawdry miracles, and has her being. Here, in sober summary, are the particulars:

1. That the house is "of conventional design."
2. That there is "a spacious areaway" between its two wings.
3. That these wings are "of cream-coloured pressed brick."
4. That the entrance between them is "protected by a handsome wrought-iron door."
5. That to either side of this door is "an electric lamp support of handsome design."
6. That in each of these lamp supports there are "lovely cream-coloured globes, shedding a soft lustre."
7. That inside is "the usual lobby."
8. That in the lobby is "the usual elevator."
9. That in the elevator is the usual "uniformed negro elevator man."
10. That this negro elevator man (name not given) is "indifferent and impertinent."
11. That a telephone switchboard is also in the lobby.
12. That the building is seven stories in height.

In "The Financier" there is the same exasperating rolling up of irrelevant facts. The court proceedings in the trial of Cowperwood are given with all the exactness of a parliamentary report in the London *Times.* The speeches of the opposing counsel are set down nearly in full, and with them the remarks of the judge, and after that the opinion of the Appellate Court on appeal, with the dissenting opinions as a sort of appendix. In "Sister Carrie" the thing is less savagely carried out, but that is not Dreiser's fault, for the manuscript was revised by some anonymous hand, and the printed version is but little more than half the length of the original. In "The Titan" and "Jennie Gerhardt" no such brake upon exuberance is visible; both books are crammed with details that serve no purpose, and are as flat as ditch-water. Even in the two volumes of personal record, "A Traveler at Forty" and "A Hoosier Holiday," there is the same furious accumulation of trivialities. Consider the former. It is without structure, without selection, without reticence. One arises from it as from a great babbling, half drunken. On the one hand the author fills a long and gloomy chapter with the story of the Borgias, apparently under the impression that it is news, and on the other hand he enters into intimate and inconsequential confidences about all the persons he meets en route, sparing neither the innocent nor the obscure. The children of his English host at Bridgely Level strike him as fantastic little creatures, even as a bit uncanny—and he duly sets it down. He meets an Englishman on a French train who pleases him much, and the two become good friends and see Rome together, but the fellow's wife is "obstreperous" and "haughty in her manner" and so "loud-spoken in her opinions" that she is "really offensive"—and down it goes. He makes an impression on a Mlle. Marcelle in Paris, and she accompanies him from Monte Carlo to Ventimiglia, and there gives him a parting kiss and whispers, "*Avril-Fontainebleau*"—and lo, this sweet one is duly spread upon the minutes. He permits himself to be arrested by a fair privateer in Piccadilly, and goes with her to one of the dens of sin that suffragettes see in their nightmares, and cross-examines her at length regarding her ancestry, her professional ethics and ideals, and her earnings at her dismal craft—and into the book goes a full report of the proceedings. He is entertained by an eminent Dutch jurist in Amsterdam—and upon the pages of the chronicle it appears that the gentleman is "waxy" and "a little pedantic," and that he is probably the sort of "thin, delicate, well barbered" professor that Ibsen had in mind when he cast about for a husband for the daughter of General Gabler.

Such is the art of writing as Dreiser understands it and practises it—an endless piling up of minutiae, an almost ferocious tracking down of ions, electrons and molecules, an unshakable determination to tell it all. One is amazed by the mole-like diligence of the man, and no less by his exasperating disregard for the ease of his readers. A Dreiser novel, at least of the later canon, cannot be read as other novels are read—on a winter evening or summer afternoon, between meal and meal, travelling from New York to Boston. It demands the attention for almost a week, and uses up the faculties for a month. If, reading "The 'Genius,'" one were to become engrossed in the fabulous manner described in the publishers' advertisements, and so find oneself unable to put it down and go to bed before the end, one would get no sleep for three days and three nights.

Worse, there are no charms of style to mitigate the rigours of these vast steppes and pampas of narration. Joseph Joubert's saying that "words should stand out well from the paper" is quite incomprehensible to Dreiser; he never imitates Flaubert by writing for "*la respiration et l'oreille.*" There is no painful groping for the inevitable word, or for what Walter Pater called "the gipsy phrase"; the common, even the commonplace, coin of speech is good enough. On the first page of "Jennie Gerhardt" one encounters "frank, open countenance," "diffident manner," "helpless poor," "untutored mind," "honest necessity," and half a dozen other stand-bys of the second-rate newspaper reporter. In "Sister Carrie" one finds "high noon," "hurrying throng," "unassuming restaurant," "dainty slippers," "high-strung nature," and "cool, calculating world"—all on a few pages. Carrie's sister, Minnie Hanson, "gets" the supper. Hanson himself is "wrapped up" in his child. Carrie decides to enter Storm and King's office, "no matter what." In "The Titan" the word "trig" is worked to death; it takes on, toward the end, the character of a banal and preposterous refrain. In the other books one encounters mates for it—words made to do duty in as many senses as the American verb "to fix" or the journalistic "to secure." . . .

I often wonder if Dreiser gets anything properly describable as pleasure out of this dogged accumulation of threadbare, undistinguished, uninspiring nouns, adjectives, verbs, adverbs, pronouns, participles and conjunctions. To the man with an ear for verbal delicacies—the man who searches painfully for the perfect word, and puts the way of saying a thing above the thing said—there is in writing the constant joy of sudden discovery, of happy accident. A phrase springs up full blown, sweet and caressing. But what joy can there be in rolling up sentences that have no more life and beauty in them, intrinsically, than so many election bulletins? Where is the thrill in the manufacture of such a paragraph as that in which Mrs. Althea Jones' sordid habitat is described with such inexorable particularity? Or in the laborious confection of such stuff as this, from Book I, Chapter IV, of "The 'Genius' "?:

> The city of Chicago—who shall portray it! This vast ruck of life that had sprung suddenly into existence upon the dank marshes of a lake shore!

Or this from the epilogue to "The Financier";

> There is a certain fish whose scientific name is *Mycteroperca Bonaci,* and whose common name is Black Grouper, which is of considerable value as an afterthought in this connection, and which deserves much to be better known. It is a healthy creature, growing quite regularly to a weight of two hundred and fifty pounds, and living a comfortable, lengthy existence because of its very remarkable ability to adapt itself to conditions. . . .

Or this from his pamphlet, "Life, Art and America": [1]

> Alas, alas! for art in America. It has a hard stubby row to hoe.

But I offer no more examples. Every reader of the Dreiser novels must cherish astounding specimens—of awkward, platitudinous marginalia, of whole scenes spoiled by bad writing, of phrases as brackish as so many lumps of sodium hyposulphite. Here and there, as in parts of "The Titan" and again in parts of "A Hoosier Holiday," an evil

[1] New York, 1917; reprinted from *The Seven Arts* for Feb., 1917.

conscience seems to haunt him and he gives hard striving to his manner, and more than once there emerges something that is almost graceful. But a backsliding always follows this phosphorescence of reform. "The 'Genius,'" coming after "The Titan," marks the high tide of his bad writing. There are passages in it so clumsy, so inept, so irritating that they seem almost unbelievable; nothing worse is to be found in the newspapers. Nor is there any compensatory deftness in structure, or solidity of design, to make up for this carelessness in detail. The well-made novel, of course, can be as hollow as the well-made play of Scribe—but let us at least have a beginning, a middle and an end! Such a story as "The 'Genius'" is as gross and shapeless as Brünnhilde. It billows and bulges out like a cloud of smoke, and its internal organization is almost as vague. There are episodes that, with a few chapters added, would make very respectable novels. There are chapters that need but a touch or two to be excellent short stories. The thing rambles, staggers, trips, heaves, pitches, struggles, totters, wavers, halts, turns aside, trembles on the edge of collapse. More than once it seems to be foundering, both in the equine and in the maritime senses. The tale has been heard of a tree so tall that it took two men to see to the top of it. Here is a novel so brobdingnagian that a single reader can scarcely read his way through it. . . .

§ 3

Of the general ideas which lie at the bottom of all of Dreiser's work it is impossible to be in ignorance, for he has exposed them at length in "A Hoosier Holiday" and summarized them in "Life, Art and America." In their main outlines they are not unlike the fundamental assumptions of Joseph Conrad. Both novelists see human existence as a seeking without a finding; both reject the prevailing interpretations of its meaning and mechanism; both take refuge in "I do not know." Put "A Hoosier Holiday" beside Conrad's "A Personal Record," and you will come upon parallels from end to end. Or better still, put it beside Hugh Walpole's "Joseph Conrad," in which the Conradean metaphysic is condensed from the novels even better than Conrad has done it himself: at once you will see how the two novelists, each a worker in the elemental emotions, each a rebel against the current assurance and superficiality, each an alien to his place and time, touch each other in a hundred ways.

"Conrad," says Walpole, "is of the firm and resolute conviction that life is too strong, too clever and too remorseless for the sons of men." And then, in amplification: "It is as though, from some high window, looking down, he were able to watch some shore, from whose security men were forever launching little cockleshell boats upon a limitless and angry sea. . . . From his height he can follow their fortunes, their brave struggles, their fortitude to the very end. He admires their courage, the simplicity of their faith, but his irony springs from his knowledge of the inevitable end." . . .

Substitute the name of Dreiser for that of Conrad, and you will have to change scarcely a word. Perhaps one, to wit, "clever." I suspect that Dreiser, writing so of his own creed, would be tempted to make it "stupid," or, at all events, "unintelligible." The struggle of man, as he sees it, is more than impotent; it is gratuitous and purposeless. There is, to his eye, no grand ingenuity, no skilful adaptation of means to end, no moral (or even dramatic) plan in the order of the universe. He can get out of it only a sense of profound and inexplicable *dis*order. The waves which batter the cockleshells change their direction at every instant. Their navigation is a vast adventure, but intolerably fortuitous and inept—a voyage without chart, compass, sun or stars. . . .

So at bottom. But to look into the blackness steadily, of course, is almost beyond the endurance of man. In the very moment that its impenetrability is grasped the imagination begins attacking it with pale beams of false light. All religions, I daresay, are thus projected from the questioning soul of man, and not only all religious, but also all great agnosticisms. Nietzsche, shrinking from the horror of that abyss of negation, revived the Pythagorean concept of *der ewigen Wiederkunft*—a vain and blood-curdling sort of comfort. To it, after a while, he added explanations almost Christian—a whole repertoire of whys and wherefores, aims and goals, aspirations and significances. The late Mark Twain, in an unpublished work, toyed with a equally daring idea: that men are to some unimaginably vast and incomprehensible Being what the unicellular organisms of his body are to man, and so on *ad infinitum*. Dreiser occasionally inclines to much the same hypothesis; he likens the endless reactions going on in the world we know, the myriadal creation, collision and destruction of entities, to the slow accumulation and organization of cells *in utero*. He would make us specks in the insentient embryo of some gigantic Presence whose form is still unimaginable and whose birth must wait for Eons and Eons. Again, he turns to something not easily distinguishable from philosophical idealism, whether out of Berkeley or Fichte it is hard to make out—that is, he would interpret the whole phenomenon of life as no more than an appearance, a nightmare of some unseen sleeper or of men themselves, an "uncanny blur of nothingness"—in Euripides' phrase, "a song sung by an idiot, dancing down the wind." Yet again, he talks vaguely of the intricate polyphony of a cosmic orchestra, cacophonous to our dull ears. Finally, he puts the observed into the ordered, reading a purpose in the displayed event: "life was intended to sting and hurt" . . . But these are only gropings, and not to be read too critically. From speculations and explanations he always returns, Conrad-like, to the bald fact: to "the spectacle and stress of life." All he can make out clearly is "a vast compulsion which has nothing to do with the individual desires or tastes or impulses of individuals." That compulsion springs "from the settling processes of forces which we do not in the least understand, over which we have no control, and in whose grip we are as grains of dust or sand, blown hither and thither, for what purpose we cannot even suspect." [1] Man is not only doomed to defeat, but denied any glimpse or un-

[1] Life, Art and America, p. 5.

derstanding of his antagonist. Here we come upon an agnosticism that has almost got beyond curiosity. What good would it do us, asks Dreiser, to know? In our ignorance and helplessness, we may at least get a slave's consolation out of cursing the unknown gods. Suppose we saw them striving blindly, too, and pitied them? . . .

But, as I say, this scepticism is often tempered by guesses at a possibly hidden truth, and the confession that this truth may exist reveals the practical unworkableness of the unconditioned system, at least for Dreiser. Conrad is far more resolute, and it is easy to see why. He is, by birth and training, an aristocrat. He has the gift of emotional detachment. The lures of facile doctrine do not move him. In his irony there is a disdain which plays about even the ironist himself. Dreiser is a product of far different forces and traditions, and is capable of no such escapement. Struggle as he may, and fume and protest as he may, he can no more shake off the chains of his intellectual and cultural heritage than he can change the shape of his nose. What that heritage is you may find out in detail by reading "A Hoosier Holiday," or in summary by glancing at the first few pages of "Life, Art and America." Briefly described, it is the burden of a believing mind, a moral attitude, a lingering superstition. One-half of the man's brain, so to speak, wars with the other half. He is intelligent, he is thoughtful, he is a sound artist—but there come moments when a dead hand falls upon him, and he is once more the Indiana peasant, snuffing absurdly over imbecile sentimentalities, giving a grave ear to quackeries, snorting and eye-rolling with the best of them. One generation spans too short a time to free the soul of man. Nietzsche, to the end of his days, remained a Prussian pastor's son, and hence two-thirds a Puritan; he erected his war upon holiness, toward the end, into a sort of holy war. Kipling, the grandson of a Methodist preacher, reveals the tin-pot evangelist with increasing clarity as youth and its ribaldries pass away and he falls back upon his fundamentals. And that other English novelist who springs from the servants' hall—let us not be surprised or blame him if he sometimes writes like a bounder.

The truth about Dreiser is that he is still in the transition stage between Christian Endeavour and civilization, between Warsaw, Indiana and the Socratic grove, between being a good American and being a free man, and so he sometimes vacillates perilously between a moral sentimentalism and a somewhat extravagant revolt. "The 'Genius,'" on the one hand, is almost a tract for rectitude, a Warning to the Young; its motto might be *Scheut die Dirnen!* And on the other hand, it is full of a laborious truculence that can only be explained by imagining the author as heroically determined to prove that he is a plain-spoken fellow and his own man, let the chips fall where they may. So, in spots, in "The Financier" and "The Titan," both of them far better books. There is an almost moral frenzy to expose and riddle what passes for morality among the stupid. The isolation of irony is never reached; the man is still evangelical; his ideas are still novelties to him; he is as solemnly absurd in some of his floutings of the Code Américain as he is in his respect for Bouguereau, or in his flirtings with the New Thought, or in his naïve belief in the importance of novel-writing. Somewhere or other I have called all this the Greenwich Village complex. It is not genuine artists, serving beauty reverently and proudly, who herd in those cockroached cellars and bawl for art; it is a mob of half-educated yokels and cockneys to whom the very idea of art is still novel, and intoxicating—and more than a little bawdy.

Not that Dreiser actually belongs to this ragamuffin company. Far from it, indeed. There is in him, hidden deep-down, a great instinctive artist, and hence the makings of an aristocrat. In his muddled way, held back by the manacles of his race and time, and his steps made uncertain by a guiding theory which too often eludes his own comprehension, he yet manages to produce works of art of unquestionable beauty and authority, and to interpret life in a manner that is poignant and illuminating. There is vastly more intuition in him than intellectualism; his talent is essentially feminine, as Conrad's is masculine; his ideas always seem to be deduced from his feelings. The view of life that got into "Sister Carrie," his first book, was not the product of a conscious thinking out of Carrie's problems. It simply got itself there by the force of the artistic passion behind it; its coherent statement had to wait for other and more reflective days. The thing began as a vision, not as a syllogism. Here the name of Franz Schubert inevitably comes up. Schubert was an ignoramus, even in music; he knew less about polyphony, which is the mother of harmony, which is the mother of music, than the average conservatory professor. But nevertheless he had such a vast instinctive sensitiveness to musical values, such a profound and accurate feeling for beauty in tone, that he not only arrived at the truth in tonal relations, but even went beyond what, in his day, was known to be the truth, and so led an advance. Likewise, Giorgione da Castelfranco and Masaccio come to mind: painters of the first rank, but untutored, unsophisticated, uncouth. Dreiser, within his limits, belongs to this cabot-shod company of the elect. One thinks of Conrad, not as artist first, but as savant. There is something of the icy aloofness of the laboratory in him, even when the images he conjures up pulsate with the very glow of life. He is almost as self-conscious as the Beethoven of the last quartets. In Dreiser the thing is more intimate, more disorderly, more a matter of pure feeling. He gets his effects, one might almost say, not by designing them, but by living them.

But whatever the process, the power of the image evoked is not to be gainsaid. It is not only brilliant on the surface, but mysterious and appealing in its depths. One swiftly forgets his intolerable writing, his mirthless, sedulous, repellent manner, in the face of the Athenian tragedy he instils into his seduced and soul-sick servant girls, his barbaric pirates of finances, his conquered and hamstrung supermen, his wives who sit and wait. He has, like Conrad, a sure talent for depicting the spirit in disintegration. Old Gerhardt, in "Jennie Gerhardt," is alone worth all the *dramatis personae* of popular American fiction since the days of "Rob o' the Bowl"; Howells could no more have created him, in his Rodinesque impudence of outline, than he could have created Tartuffe or Gargantua. Such a novel as "Sister Carrie" stands quite outside the brief traffic of the customary stage. It leaves behind it an unescapable impression of bigness, of epic sweep and dignity. It is not a mere story, not a novel in the customary American meaning of the word; it is at once a psalm of life and a criticism of life—and that criticism loses nothing by the fact that its burden is despair. Here, precisely, is the point of Dreiser's departure from his fellows. He puts into his novels a touch of the eternal *Weltschmerz*. They get below the drama that is of the moment and reveal the greater drama that is without end. They arouse those deep and lasting emotions which grow out of the recognition of elemental and universal tragedy. His aim is not merely to tell a tale; his aim is to show the vast ebb and flow of forces which sway and condition human destiny. One cannot imagine him consenting to Conan Doyle's statement of the purpose of fiction, quoted with characteristic approval by the New York *Times*: "to amuse mankind, to help the sick and the dull and the weary." Nor is his purpose to instruct; if he is a pedagogue it is only incidentally and as a weakness. The thing he seeks to do is to stir, to awaken, to move. One does not arise from such a book as "Sister Carrie" with a smirk of satisfaction; one leaves it infinitely touched.

§ 4

It is, indeed, a truly amazing first book, and one marvels to hear that it was begun lightly. Dreiser in those days (*circa* 1899), had seven or eight years of newspaper work behind him, in Chicago, St. Louis, Toledo, Cleveland, Buffalo, Pittsburgh and New York, and was beginning to feel that reaction of disgust which attacks all newspaper men when the enthusiasm of youth wears out. He had been successful, but he saw how hollow that success was, and how little surety it held out for the future. The theatre was what chiefly lured him; he had written plays in his nonage, and he now proposed to do them on a large scale, and so get some of the easy dollars of Broadway. It was an old friend from Toledo, Arthur Henry, who turned him toward story-writing. The two had met while Henry was city editor of the *Blade*, and Dreiser a reporter looking for a job.[1] A firm friendship sprang up, and Henry conceived a high opinion of Dreiser's ability,

[1] The episode is related in A Hoosier Holiday.

and urged him to try a short story. Dreiser was distrustful of his own skill, but Henry kept at him, and finally, during a holiday the two spent together at Maumee, Ohio, he made the attempt. Henry had the manuscript typewritten and sent it to *Ainslee's Magazine.* A week or so later there came a cheque for $75.

This was in 1898. Dreiser wrote four more stories during the year following, and sold them all. Henry now urged him to attempt a novel, but again his distrust of himself held him back. Henry finally tried a rather unusual argument: he had a novel of his own on the stocks,[1] and he represented that he was in difficulties with it and in need of company. One day, in September, 1899, Dreiser took a sheet of yellow paper and wrote a title at random. That title was "Sister Carrie," and with no more definite plan than the mere name offered the book began. It went ahead steadily enough until the middle of October, and had come by then to the place where Carrie meets Hurstwood. At that point Dreiser left it in disgust. It seemed pitifully dull and inconsequential, and for two months he put the manuscript away. Then, under renewed urgings by Henry, he resumed the writing, and kept on to the place where Hurstwood steals

[1] A Princess of Arcady, published in 1900.

the money. Here he went aground upon a comparatively simple problem; he couldn't devise a way to manage the robbery. Late in January he gave it up. But the faithful Henry kept urging him, and in March he resumed work, and soon had the story finished. The latter part, despite many distractions, went quickly. Once the manuscript was complete, Henry suggested various cuts, and in all about 40,000 words came out. The fair copy went to the Harpers. They refused it without ceremony and soon afterward Dreiser carried the manuscript to Doubleday, Page & Co. He left it with Frank Doubleday, and before long there came notice of its acceptance, and, what is more, a contract. But after the story was in type it fell into the hands of the wife of one of the members of the firm, and she conceived so strong a notion of its immorality that she soon convinced her husband and his associates. There followed a series of acrimonious negotiations, with Dreiser holding resolutely to the letter of his contract. It was at this point that Frank Norris entered the combat—bravely but in vain. The pious Barabbases, confronted by their signature, found it impossible to throw up the book entirely, but there was no nomination in the bond regarding either the style of binding or the number of copies to be issued, and so they evaded further dispute by bringing out the book in a very small edition and with modest unstamped covers. Copies of this edition are now eagerly sought by book-collectors, and one in good condition fetches $25 or more in the auction rooms. Even the second edition (1907), bearing the imprint of B. W. Dodge & Co., carries an increasing premium.

The passing years work strange farces. The Harpers, who had refused "Sister Carrie" with a spirit bordering upon indignation in 1900, took over the rights of publication from B. W. Dodge & Co., in 1912, and reissued the book in a new (and extremely hideous) format, with a publisher's note containing smug quotations from the encomiums of the *Fortnightly Review*, the *Athenaeum*, the *Spectator*, the *Academy* and other London critical journals. More, they contrived humorously to push the date of their copyright back to 1900. But this new enthusiasm for artistic freedom did not last long. They had published "Jennie Gerhardt" in 1911 and they did "The Financier" in 1912, but when "The Titan" followed, in 1914, they were seized with qualms, and suppressed the book after it had got into type. In this emergency the English firm of John Lane came to the rescue, only to seek cover itself when the Comstocks attacked "The

'Genius,' " two years later. . . . For his high services to American letters, Walter H. Page, of Doubleday, Page & Co., was made ambassador to England, where "Sister Carrie" is regarded (according to the Harpers), as "the best story, on the whole, that has yet come out of America." A curious series of episodes. Another proof, perhaps, of that cosmic imbecility upon which Dreiser is so fond of discoursing. . . .

But of all this I shall say more later on, when I come to discuss the critical reception of the Dreiser novels, and the efforts made by the New York Society for the Suppression of Vice to stop their sale. The thing to notice here is that the author's difficulties with "Sister Carrie" came within an ace of turning him from novel-writing completely. Stray copies of the suppressed first edition, true enough, fell into the hands of critics who saw the story's value, and during the first year or two of the century it enjoyed a sort of esoteric vogue, and encouragement came from unexpected sources. Moreover, a somewhat bowdlerized English edition, published by William Heinemann in 1901, made a fair success, and even provoked a certain mild controversy. But the author's income from the book remained almost *nil,* and so he was forced to seek a livelihood in other directions. His history during the next ten years belongs to the tragi-comedy of letters. For five of them he was a Grub Street hack, turning his hand to any literary job that offered. He wrote short stories for the popular magazines, or special articles, or poems, according as their needs varied. He concocted fabulous tales for the illustrated supplements of the Sunday newspapers. He rewrote the bad stuff of other men. He returned to reporting. He did odd pieces of editing. He tried his hand at one-act plays. He even ventured upon advertisement writing. And all the while, the best that he could get out of his industry was a meagre living.

In 1905, tiring of the uncertainties of this life, he accepted a post on the staff of Street & Smith, the millionaire publishers of cheap magazines, servant-girl romances and dime-novels, and here, in the very slums of letters, he laboured with tongue in cheek until the next year. The tale of his duties will fill, I daresay, a volume or two in the autobiography on which he is said to be working; it is a chronicle full of achieved impossibilities. One of his jobs, for example, was to reduce a whole series of dime-novels, each 60,000 words in length, to 30,000 words apiece. He accomplished it by cutting each one into halves, and writing a new ending for the first half and a new beginning for the second, with new titles for both. This doubling of their property aroused the admiration of his employers; they promised him an assured and easy future in the dime-novel business. But he tired of it, despite this revelation of a gift for it, and in 1906 he became managing editor of the *Broadway Magazine,* then struggling into public notice. A year later he transferred his flag to the Butterick Building, and became chief editor of the *Delineator,* the *Designer* and other such gospels for the fair. Here, of course, he was as much out of water as in the dime-novel foundry of Street & Smith, but at all events the pay was good, and there was a certain leisure at the end of the day's work. In 1907, as part of his duties, he organized the National Child Rescue Campaign, which still rages as the *Delineator's* contribution to the Uplift. At about the same time he began "Jennie Gerhardt." It is curious to note that, during these same years, Arnold Bennett was slaving in London as the editor of *Woman.*

Dreiser left the *Delineator* in 1910, and for the next half year or so endeavoured to pump vitality into the *Bohemian Magazine,* in which he had acquired a proprietary interest. But the *Bohemian* soon departed this life, carrying some of his savings with it, and he gave over his enforced leisure to "Jennie Gerhardt," completing the book in 1911. Its publication by the Harpers during the same year worked his final emancipation from the editorial desk. It was praised, and what is more, it sold, and royalties began to come in. A new edition of "Sister Carrie" followed in 1912, with "The Financier" hard upon its heels. Since then Dreiser has devoted himself wholly to serious work. "The Financier" was put forth as the first volume of "a trilogy of desire"; the second volume, "The Titan," was published in 1914; the third is yet to come. "The 'Genius' " appeared in 1915; "The Bulwark" is just announced. In 1912, accompanied by Grant Richards, the London publisher, Dreiser made his first trip abroad, visiting England, France, Italy and Germany. His impressions were recorded in "A Traveler at Forty," published in 1913. In the summer of 1915, accompanied by Franklin Booth, the illustrator, he made an automobile journey to his old haunts in Indiana, and the record is in "A Hoosier Holiday," published in 1916. His other writings include a volume of "Plays of the Natural and the Supernatural" (1916); "Life, Art and America," a pamphlet against Puritanism in letters (1917); a dozen or more short stories and novelettes, a few poems, and a three-act drama, "The Hand of the Potter."

Dreiser was born at Terre Haute, Indiana, on August 27, 1871, and, like most of us, is of mongrel blood, with the German, perhaps, predominating. He is a tall man, awkward in movement and nervous in habit; the boon of beauty has been denied him. The history of his youth is set forth in full in "A Hoosier Holiday." It is curious to note that he is a brother to the late Paul Dresser, author of "The Banks of the Wabash" and other popular songs, and that he himself, helping Paul over a hard place, wrote the affecting chorus:

Oh, the moon is fair tonight along the Wabash,
From the fields there comes the breath of new-mown hay;
Through the sycamores the candle lights are gleaming . . .

But no doubt you know it.

§ 5

The work of Dreiser, considered as craftsmanship pure and simple, is extremely uneven, and the distance separating his best from his worst is almost infinite. It is difficult to believe that the novelist who wrote certain extraordinarily vivid chapters in "Jennie Gerhardt," and "A Hoosier Holiday," and, above all, in "The Titan," is the same who achieved the unescapable dulness of parts of "The Financier" and the general stupidity and stodginess of

"The 'Genius.'" Moreover, the tide of his writing does not rise or fall with any regularity; he neither improves steadily nor grows worse steadily. Only half an eye is needed to see the superiority of "Jennie Gerhardt," as a sheer piece of writing, to "Sister Carrie," but on turning to "The Financier," which followed "Jennie Gerhardt" by an interval of but one year, one observes a falling off which, at its greatest, is almost indistinguishable from a collapse. "Jennie Gerhardt" is suave, persuasive, well-ordered, solid in structure, instinct with life. "The Financier," for all its merits in detail, is loose, tedious, vapid, exasperating. But had any critic, in the autumn of 1912, argued thereby that Dreiser was finished, that he had shot his bolt, his discomfiture would have come swiftly, for "The Titan," which followed in 1914, was almost as well done as "The Financier" had been ill done, and there are parts of it which remain, to this day, the very best writing that Dreiser has ever achieved. But "The 'Genius'"? Ay, in "The 'Genius'" the pendulum swings back again! It is flaccid, elephantine, doltish, coarse, dismal, flatulent, sophomoric, ignorant, unconvincing, wearisome. One pities the jurisconsult who is condemned, by Comstockian clamour, to plough through such a novel. In it there is a sort of humourless *reductio ad ab-*

surdum, not only of the Dreiser manner, but even of certain salient tenets of the Dreiser philosophy. At its best it has a moral flavour. At its worst it is almost maudlin. . . .

The most successful of the Dreiser novels, judged by sales, is "Sister Carrie," and the causes thereof are not far to seek. On the one hand, its suppression in 1900 gave it a whispered fame that was converted into a public celebrity when it was republished in 1907, and on the other hand it shares with "Jennie Gerhardt" the capital advantage of having a young and appealing woman for its chief figure. The sentimentalists thus have a heroine to cry over, and to put into a familiar pigeon-hole; Carrie becomes a sort of Pollyanna. More, it is, at bottom, a tale of love—the one theme of permanent interest to the average American novel-reader, the chief stuffing of all our best-selling romances. True enough, it is vastly more than this—there is in it, for example, the astounding portrait of Hurstwood—, but it seems to me plain that its relative popularity is by no means a test of its relative merit, and that the causes of that popularity must be sought in other directions. Its defect, as a work of art, is a defect of structure. Like Norris' "McTeague" it has a broken back. In the midst of the story of Carrie, Dreiser pauses to tell the story of Hurstwood—a memorably vivid and tragic story, to be sure, but still one that, considering artistic form and organization, does damage to the main business of the book. Its outstanding merit is its simplicity, its unaffected seriousness and fervour, the spirit of youth that is in it. One feels that it was written, not by a novelist conscious of his tricks, but by a novice carried away by his own flaming eagerness, his own high sense of the interest of what he was doing. In this aspect, it is perhaps more typically Dreiserian than any of its successors. And maybe we may seek here for a good deal of its popular appeal, for there is a contagion in naïveté as in enthusiasm, and the simple novel-reader may recognize the kinship of a simple mind in the novelist.

But it is in "Jennie Gerhardt" that Dreiser first shows his true mettle. . . . "The power to tell the same story in two forms," said George Moore, "is the sign of the true artist." Here Dreiser sets himself that difficult task, and here he carries it off with almost complete success. Reduce the story to a hundred words, and the same words would also describe "Sister Carrie." Jennie, like Carrie, is a rose grown from turnip-seed. Over each, at the start, hangs poverty, ignorance, the dumb helplessness of the Shudra, and yet in each there is that indescribable something, that element of essential gentleness, that innate inward beauty which levels all barriers of caste, and makes Esther a fit queen for Ahasuerus. Some Frenchman has put it into a phrase: *"Une âme grande dans un petit destin"* —a great soul in a small destiny. Jennie has some touch of that greatness; Dreiser is forever calling her " a big woman"; it is a refrain almost as irritating as the "trig" of "The Titan." Carrie, one feels, is of baser metal; her dignity never rises to anything approaching nobility. But the history of each is the history of the other. Jennie, like Carrie, escapes from the physical miseries of the struggle for existence only to taste the worse miseries of the struggle for happiness. Don't mistake me; we have here no maudlin tales of seduced maidens. Seduction, in truth, is far from tragedy for either Jennie or Carrie. The gain of each, until the actual event has been left behind and obliterated by experiences more salient and poignant, is greater than her loss, and that gain is to the soul as well as to the creature. With the rise from want to security, from fear to ease, comes an awakening of the finer perceptions, a widening of the sympathies, a gradual unfolding of the delicate flower called personality, an increased capacity for loving and living. But with all this, and as a part of it, there comes, too, an increased capacity for suffering—and so in the end, when love slips away and the empty years stretch before, it is the awakened and supersentient woman that pays for the folly of the groping, bewildered girl. The tragedy of Carrie and Jennie, in brief, is not that they are degraded, but that they are lifted up, not that they go to the gutter, but that they escape the gutter and glimpse the stars.

But if the two stories are thus variations upon the same sombre theme, if each starts from the same place and arrives at the same dark goal, if each shows a woman heartened by the same hopes and tortured by the same agonies, there is still a vast difference between them, and that difference is the measure of the author's progress in his craft during the eleven years between 1900 and 1911. "Sister Carrie," at bottom, is no more than a first sketch, a rough piling up of observations and ideas, disordered and often incoherent. In the midst of the story, as I have said, the author forgets it, and starts off upon another. In "Jennie Gerhardt" there is no such flaccidity of structure, no such vacillation in aim, no such proliferation of episode. Considering that it is by Dreiser, it is extraordinarily adept and intelligent in design; only in "The Titan" has he ever done so well. From beginning to end the narrative flows logically, steadily, congruously. Episodes there are, of course, but they keep their proper place and bulk. It is always Jennie that stands at the centre of the traffic; it is in Jennie's soul that every scene is ultimately played out. Her father and mother; Senator Brander, the god of her first worship; her daughter Vesta, and Lester Kane, the man who makes and mars her—all these are drawn with infinite painstaking, and in every one of them there is the blood of life. But it is Jennie that dominates the drama from curtain to curtain. Not an event is unrelated to her; not a climax fails to make clearer the struggles going on in her mind and heart.

It is in "Jennie Gerhardt" that Dreiser's view of life begins to take on coherence and to show a general tendency. In "Sister Carrie" the thing is still chiefly representation and no more; the image is undoubtedly vivid, but its significance, in the main, is left undisplayed. In "Jennie Gerhardt" this pictorial achievement is reinforced by interpretation; one carries away an impression that something has been said; it is not so much a visual image of Jennie that remains as a sense of the implacable tragedy that engulfs her. The book is full of artistic passion. It lives and glows. It awakens recognition and feeling. Its lucid ideational structure, even more than the artless gusto of "Sister Carrie," produces a penetrating and powerful effect. Jennie is no mere individual; she is a type of the national character, almost the archetype of the muddled, aspiring, tragic, fate-flogged mass. And the scene in which she is set is brilliantly national too. The Chicago of those great days of feverish money-grabbing and crazy aspiration may well stand as the epitome of America, and it is made clearer here than in any other American novel—clearer than in "The Pit" or "The Cliff-Dwellers"—clearer than in any book by an Easterner—almost as clear as the Paris of Balzac and Zola. Finally, the style of the story is indissolubly wedded to its matter. The narrative, in places, has an almost scriptural solemnity; in its very harshness and baldness there is something subtly meet and fitting. One cannot imagine such a history done in the strained phrases of Meredith or the fugal manner of Henry James. One cannot imagine that stark, stenographic dialogue adorned with the tinsel of pretty words. The thing, to reach the heights it touches, could have been done only in the way it has been done. As it stands, I would not take anything away from it, not even its journalistic banalities, its lack of humour, its incessant returns to C major. A primitive and touching poetry is in it. It is a novel, I am convinced, of the first consideration. . . .

In "The Financier" this poetry is almost absent, and that fact is largely to blame for the book's lack of charm. By the time we see him in "The Titan" Frank Cowperwood has taken on heroic proportions and the romance of great adventure is in him, but in "The Financier" he is still little more than an extra-pertinacious money-grubber, and not unrelated to the average stock broker or corner grocer. True enough, Dreiser says specifically that he is more, that the thing he craves is not money but power—power to force lesser men to execute his commands, power to surround himself with beautiful and splendid things, power to amuse himself with women, power to defy and nullify the laws made for the timorous and unimaginative. But the intent of the author never really gets into his picture. His Cowperwood in this first stage is hard, commonplace, unimaginative. In "The Titan" he flowers out as a blend of revolutionist and voluptuary, a highly civilized Lorenzo the Magnificent, an immoralist who would not hesitate two minutes about seducing a saint, but would turn sick at the thought of harming a child. But in "The Financier" he is still in the larval state, and a repellent sordidness hangs about him.

Moreover, the story of his rise is burdened by two defects which still further corrupt its effect. One lies in the fact that Dreiser is quite unable to get the feel, so to speak, of Philadelphia, just as he is unable to get the feel of New York in "The 'Genius.'" The other is that the style of the writing in the book reduces the dreiserian manner to absurdity, and almost to impossibility. The incredibly lazy, involved and unintelligent description of the trial of Cowperwood I have already mentioned. We get, in this lumbering chronicle, not a cohesive and luminous picture, but a dull, photographic representation of the whole tedious process, beginning with an account of the political obligations of the judge and district attorney, proceeding to a consideration of the habits of mind of each of the twelve jurymen, and ending with a summary of the majority and minority opinions of the court of appeals, and a discussion of the motives, ideals, traditions, prejudices, sympathies and chicaneries behind them, each and severally. When Cowperwood goes into the market, his operations are set forth in their last detail; we are told how many shares he buys, how much he pays for them, what the commission is, what his profit comes to. When he comes into chance contact with a politician, we hear all about that politician, including his family affairs. When he builds and furnishes a house, the chief rooms in it are inventoried with such care that not a chair or a rug or a picture on the wall is overlooked. The endless piling up of such non-essentials cripples and incommodes the story; its drama is too copiously swathed in words to achieve a sting; the Dreiser manner devours and defeats itself.

But none the less the book has compensatory merits. Its character sketches, for all the cloud of words, are lucid and vigorous. Out of that enormous complex of crooked politics and crookeder finance, Cowperwood himself stands out in the round, comprehensible and alive. And all the others, in their lesser measures, are done almost as well—Cowperwood's pale wife, whimpering in her empty house; Aileen Butler, his mistress; his doddering and eternally amazed old father; his old-fashioned, stupid, sentimental mother; Stener, the City Treasurer, a dish-rag in the face of danger; old Edward Malia Butler, that barbarian in a boiled shirt, with his Homeric hatred and his broken heart. Particularly old Butler. The years pass and he must be killed and put away, but not many readers of the book, I take it, will soon forget him. Dreiser is at his best, indeed, when he deals with old men. In their tragic helplessness they stand as symbols of that unfathomable cosmic cruelty which he sees as the motive power of life itself. More, even, than his women, he makes them poignant, vivid, memorable. The picture of old Gerhardt is full of a subtle brightness, though he is always in the background, as cautious and penny-wise as an ancient crow, trotting to his Lutheran church, pathetically ill-used by the world he never understands. Butler is another such, different in externals, but at bottom the same dismayed, questioning, pathetic old man. . . .

In "The Titan" there is a tightening of the screws, a clarifying of the action, an infinite improvement in the manner. The book, in truth, has the air of a new and clearer thinking out of "The Financier," as "Jennie Gerhardt" is a new thinking out of "Sister Carrie." With almost the same materials, the thing is given a new harmony and unity, a new plausibility, a new passion and purpose. In "The Financier" the artistic voluptuary is almost completely overshadowed by the dollar-chaser; in "The Titan" we begin to see clearly that grand battle between artist and man of money, idealist and materialist, spirit and flesh, which is the informing theme of the whole trilogy. The conflict that makes the drama, once chiefly external, now becomes more and more internal; it is played out within the soul of the man himself. The result is a character sketch of the highest colour and brilliance, a superb portrait of a complex and extremely fascinating man. Of all the personages in the Dreiser books, the Cowperwood of "The Titan" is perhaps the most radiantly real. He is accounted for in every detail, and yet, in the end, he is not accounted for at all; there hangs about him, to the last, that baffling mysteriousness which hangs about those we know most intimately. There is in him a complete and indubitable masculinity, as the eternal feminine is in Jennie. His struggle with the inexorable forces that urge him on as with whips, and lure him with false lights, and bring him to disillusion and dismay, is as typical as hers is, and as tragic. In his ultimate disaster, so plainly foreshadowed at the close, there is the clearest of all projections of the ideas that lie at the bottom of all Dreiser's work. Cowperwood, above any of them, is his protagonist.

The story, in its plan, is as transparent as in its burden. It has an austere simplicity in the telling that fits the directness of the thing told. Dreiser, as if to clear decks, throws over all the immemorial baggage of the novelist, making short shrift of "heart interest," conventional "sympathy," and even what ordinarily passes for romance. In "Sister Carrie," as I have pointed out, there is still a sweet dish for the sentimentalists; if they don't like the history of Carrie as a work of art they may still wallow in it as a sad, sad love story. Carrie is appealing, melting; she moves, like Marguerite Gautier, in an atmosphere of romantic depression. And Jennie Gerhardt, in this aspect, is merely Carrie done over—a Carrie more carefully and objectively drawn, perhaps, but still conceivably to be mistaken for a "sympathetic" heroine in a best-seller. A lady eating chocolates might jump from "Laddie" to "Jennie Gerhardt" without knowing that she was jumping ten thousand miles. The tear jugs are there to cry into. Even in "The Financier" there is still a hint of familiar things. The first Mrs. Cowperwood is sorely put upon; old Butler has the markings of an irate father; Cowperwood himself suffers the orthodox injustice and languishes in a cell. But no one, I venture, will ever fall into any such mistake in identity in approaching "The Titan." Not a single appeal to facile sentiment is in it. It proceeds from beginning to end in a forthright, uncompromising, confident manner. It is an almost purely objective account, as devoid of cheap heroics as a death certificate, of a strong man's contest with incontestable powers without and no less incontestable powers within. There is nothing of the conventional outlaw about him; he does not wear a red sash and bellow for liberty; fate wrings from him no melodramatic defiances. In the midst of the battle he views it with a sort of ironical detachment, as if lifted above himself by the sheer aesthetic spectacle. Even in disaster he asks for no quarter, no generosity, no compassion. Up or down, he keeps his zest for the game that is being played, and is sufficient unto himself.

Such a man as this Cowperwood of the Chicago days, described romantically, would be indistinguishable from the wicked earls and seven-foot guardsmen of Ouida, Robert W. Chambers and The Duchess. But described realistically and cold-bloodedly, with all that wealth of minute and apparently inconsequential detail which Dreiser piles up so amazingly, he becomes a figure astonishingly vivid, lifelike and engrossing. He fits into no *a priori* theory of conduct or scheme of rewards and punishments; he proves nothing and teaches nothing; the forces which move him are never obvious and frequently unintelligible. But in the end he seems genuinely a man—a man of the sort we see about us in the real world—not a patent and automatic fellow, reacting docilely and according to a formula, but a bundle of complexities and contradictions, a creature oscillating between the light and the shadow—at bottom, for all his typical representation of a race and a civilization, a unique and inexplicable personality. More, he is a man of the first class, an Achilles of his world; and here the achievement of Dreiser is most striking, for he succeeds where all fore-runners failed. It is easy enough to explain how John Smith courted his wife, and even how William Brown fought and died for his country, but it is inordinately difficult to give plausibility to the motives, feelings and processes of mind of a man whose salient character is that they transcend all ordinary experience. Too often, even when made by the highest creative and interpretative talent, the effort has resolved itself into a begging of the question. Shakespeare made Hamlet comprehensible to the groundlings by diluting that half of him which was Shakespeare with a half which was a college sophomore. In the same way he saved Lear by making him, in large part, a tedious and obscene old donkey—the blood brother of any average ancient of any average English taproom. Tackling Caesar, he was rescued by Brutus' knife. George Bernard Shaw, facing the same difficulty, resolved it by drawing a composite portrait of two or three London actor-managers and half a dozen English politicians. But Dreiser makes no such compromise. He bangs into the difficulties of his problem head on, and if he does not solve it absolutely, he at least makes an extraordinarily close approach to a solution. In "The Financier" a certain incredulity still hangs about Cowperwood; in "The Titan" he suddenly comes unquestionably real. If you want to get the true measure of this feat, put it beside the failure of Frank Norris with Curtis Jadwin in "The Pit." . . .

"The 'Genius,'" which interrupted the "trilogy of desire," marks the nadir of Dreiser's accomplishment, as "The Titan" marks its apogee. The plan of it, of course, is simple enough, and it is one that Dreiser, at his best, might have carried out with undoubted success. What he is trying to show, in brief, is the battle that goes on in the soul of every man of active mind between the desire for self-expression and the desire for safety, for public respect, for emotional equanimity. It is, in a sense, the story of Cowperwood told over again, but with an important difference, for Eugene Witla is a much less self-reliant and powerful fellow than Cowperwood, and so he is unable to muster up the vast resolution of spirits that he needs to attain happiness. "The Titan" is the history of a strong man. "The 'Genius'" is the history of a man essentially weak. Eugene Witla can never quite choose his route in life. He goes on sacrificing ease to aspiration and aspiration to ease to the end of the chapter. He vacillates abominably and forever between two irreconcilable desires. Even when, at the close, he sinks into a whining sort of resignation, the proud courage of Cowperwood is not in him; he is always a bit despicable in his pathos.

As I say, a story of simple outlines, and well adapted to the dreiserian pen. But it is spoiled and made a mock of by a donkeyish solemnity of attack which leaves it, on the one hand, diffuse, spineless and shapeless, and on the other hand, a compendium of platitudes. It is as if Dreiser, suddenly discovering himself a sage, put off the high passion of the artist and took to pounding a pulpit. It is almost as if he deliberately essayed upon a burlesque of himself. The book is an endless emission of the obvious, with touches of the scandalous to light up its killing monotony. It runs to 736 pages of small type; its reading is an unbearable weariness to the flesh; in the midst of it one has forgotten the beginning and is unconcerned about the end. Mingled with all the folderol, of course, there is stuff of nobler quality. Certain chapters stick in the memory; whole episodes lift themselves to the fervid luminosity of "Jennie Gerhardt"; there are character sketches that deserve all praise; one often pulls up with a reminder that the thing is the work of a proficient craftsman. But in the main it lumbers and jolts, wabbles and bores. A sort of ponderous imbecility gets into it. Both in its elaborate devices to shake up the pious and its imposing demonstrations of what every one knows, it somehow suggests the advanced thinking of Greenwich Village. I suspect, indeed, that the *vin rouge* was in Dreiser's arteries as he concocted it. He was at the intellectual menopause, and looking back somewhat wistfully and attitudinizingly toward the goatish days that were no more.

But let it go! A novelist capable of "Jennie Gerhardt" has rights, privileges, prerogatives. He may, if he will, go on a spiritual drunk now and then, and empty the stale bilges of his soul. Thackeray, having finished "Vanity Fair" and "Pendennis," bathed himself in the sheep's milk of "The Newcomes," and after "The Virginians" he did "The Adventures of Philip." Zola, with "Germinal," "La Débâcle" and "La Terre" behind him, recreated himself horribly with "Fécondité." Tolstoi, after "Anna Karenina," wrote "What Is Art?" Ibsen, after "Et Dukkehjem" and "Gengangere," wrote "Vildanden." The good God himself, after all the magnificence of Kings and Chronicles, turned Dr. Frank Crane and so botched his Writ with Proverbs. . . . A weakness that we must allow for. Whenever Dreiser, abandoning his fundamental scepticism, yields to the irrepressible human (and perhaps also divine) itch to label, to moralize, to teach, he becomes a bit absurd. Observe "The 'Genius,' " and parts of "A Hoosier Holiday" and of "A Traveler at Forty," and of "Plays of the Natural and the Supernatural." But in this very absurdity, it seems to me, there is a subtle proof that his fundamental scepticism is sound. . . .

I mention the "Plays of the Natural and the Supernatural." They are ingenious and sometimes extremely effective, but their significance is not great. The two that are "of the natural" are "The Girl in the Coffin" and "Old Ragpicker," the first a laborious evocation of the gruesome, too long by half, and the other an experiment in photographic realism, with a pair of policemen as its protagonists. All five plays "of the supernatural" follow a single plan. In the foreground, as it were, we see a sordid drama played out on the human plane, and in the background (or in the empyrean above, as you choose) we see the operation of the god-like imbecilities which sway and flay us all. The technical trick is well managed. It would be easy for such four-dimensional pieces to fall into burlesque, but in at least two cases, to wit, in "The Blue Sphere" and "In the Dark," they go off with an air. Superficially, these plays "of the supernatural" seem to show an abandonment to the wheezy, black bombazine mysticism which crops up toward the end of "The 'Genius.' " But that mysticism, at bottom, is no more than the dreiserian scepticism made visible. "For myself," says Dreiser somewhere, "I do not know what truth is, what beauty is, what love is, what hope is." And in another place: "I admit a vast compulsion which has nothing to do with the individual desires or tastes or impulses." The jokers behind the arras pull the strings. It is pretty, but what is it all about? . . . The criticism which deals only with externals sees "Sister Carrie" as no more than a deft adventure into realism. Dreiser is praised, when he is praised at all, for making Carrie so clear, for understanding her so well. But the truth is, of course, that his achievement consists precisely in making patent the impenetrable mystery of her, and of the tangled complex of striving and aspiration of which she is so helplessly a part. It is in this sense that "Sister Carrie" is a profound work. It is not a book of glib explanations, of ready formulae; it is, above all else, a book of wonder. . . .

Of "A Traveler at Forty" I have spoken briefly. It is heavy with the obvious; the most interesting thing in it is the fact that Dreiser had never seen St. Peter's or Piccadilly Circus until he was too old for either reverence or romance. "A Hoosier Holiday" is far more illuminating, despite its platitudinizing. Slow in tempo, discursive, reflective, intimate, the book covers a vast territory, and lingers in pleasant fields. One finds in it an almost complete confession of faith, artistic, religious, even political. And not infrequently that confession takes the form of ingenuous confidences—about the fortunes of the house of Dreiser, the dispersed Dreiser clan, the old neighbours in Indiana, new friends made along the way. In "A Traveler at Forty" Dreiser is surely frank enough in his vivisections; he seldom forgets a vanity or a wart. In "A Hoosier Holiday" he goes even further; he speculates heavily about all his *dramatis personae*, prodding into the motives behind their acts, wondering what they would do in this or that situation, forcing them painfully into laboratory jars. They become, in the end, not unlike characters in a novel; one misses only the neatness of a plot. Strangely enough, the one personage of the chronicle who remains dim throughout is the artist, Franklin Booth, Dreiser's host and companion on the long motor ride from New York to Indiana, and the maker of the book's excellent pictures. One gets a brilliant etching of Booth's father, and scarcely less vivid portraits of Speed, the chauffeur; of various persons encountered on the way, and of friends and relatives dredged up out of the abyss of the past. But of Booth one learns little save that he is a Christian Scientist and a fine figure of a man. There must have been much talk during those two weeks of careening along the high-road, and Booth must have borne some part in it, but what he said is very meagrely reported, and so he is still somewhat vague at the end—a personality sensed but scarcely apprehended.

However, it is Dreiser himself who is the chief character of the story, and who stands out from it most brilliantly. One sees in the man all the special marks of the novelist: his capacity for photographic and relentless observation, his insatiable curiosity, his keen zest in life as a spectacle, his comprehension of and sympathy for the poor striving of humble folks, his endless mulling of insoluble problems, his recurrent Philistinism, his impatience of restraints, his fascinated suspicion of messiahs, his passion for physical beauty, his relish for the gaudy drama of big cities; his incurable Americanism. The panorama that he enrols runs the whole scale of the colours; it is a series of extraordinarily vivid pictures. The sombre gloom of the Pennsylvania hills, with Wilkes-Barre lying among them like a gem; the procession of little country towns, sleepy and a bit hoggish; the flash of Buffalo, Cleveland, Indianapolis; the gargantuan coal-pockets and ore-docks along the Erie shore; the tinsel summer resorts; the lush Indiana farmlands, with their stodgy, bovine people—all of these things are sketched in simply, and yet almost magnificently. I know, indeed, of no book which better describes the American hinterland. Here we have no idle spying by a stranger, but a full-length representation by one who knows the thing he describes intimately, and is himself a part of it. Almost every mile of the road travelled has been Dreiser's own road in life. He knew those unkempt Indiana towns in boyhood; he wandered in the Indiana woods; he came to Toledo, Cleveland, Buffalo as a young man; all the roots of his existence are out there. And so he does his chronicle *con amore*, with many a sentimental dredging up of old memories, old hopes and old dreams.

Save for passages in "The Titan," "A Hoosier Holiday" marks the high tide of Dreiser's writing

—that is, as sheer writing. His old faults are in it, and plentifully. There are empty, brackish phrases enough, God knows—"high noon" among them. But for all that, there is an undeniable glow in it; it shows, in more than one place, an approach to style; the mere wholesaler of words has become, in some sense a connoisseur, even a voluptuary. The picture of Wilkes-Barre girt in by her hills is simply done, and yet there is imagination in it, and touches of brilliance. The sombre beauty of the Pennsylvania mountains is vividly transferred to the page. The towns by the wayside are differentiated, swiftly drawn, made to live. There are excellent sketches of people—a courtly hotelkeeper in some God-forsaken hamlet, his self-respect triumphing over his wallow; a group of babbling Civil War veterans, endlessly mouthing incomprehensible jests; the half-grown beaux and belles of the summer resorts, enchanted and yet a bit staggered by the awakening of sex; Booth *père* and his sinister politics; broken and forgotten men in the Indiana towns; policemen, waitresses, farmers, country characters; Dreiser's own people—the boys and girls of his youth; his brother Paul, the Indiana Schneckenburger and Francis Scott Key; his sisters and brothers; his beaten, hopeless, pious father; his brave and noble mother. The book is dedicated to this mother, now long dead, and in a way it is a memorial to her, a monument to affection. Life bore upon her cruelly; she knew poverty at its lowest ebb and despair at its bitterest; and yet there was in her a touch of fineness that never yielded, a gallant spirit that faced and fought things through. One thinks, somehow, of the mother of Gounod. . . . Her son has not forgotten her. His book is her epitaph. He enters into her presence with love and with reverence and with something not far from awe. . . .

As for the rest of the Dreiser compositions, I leave them to your curiosity.

§ 6

Dr. William Lyon Phelps, the Lampson professor of English language and literature at Yale, opens his chapter on Mark Twain in his "Essays on Modern Novelists" with a humorous account of the critical imbecility which pursued Mark in his own country down to his last years. The favourite national critics of that era (and it extended to 1895, at the least) were wholly blind to the fact that he was a great artist. They admitted him, somewhat grudgingly, a certain low dexterity as a clown, but that he was an imaginative writer of the first rank, or even of the fifth rank, was something that, in their insanest moments, never so much as occurred to them. Phelps cites, in particular, an ass named Professor Richardson, whose "American Literature," it appears, "is still a standard work" and "a deservedly high authority"—apparently in colleges. In the 1892 edition of this *magnum opus*, Mark is dismissed with less than four lines, and ranked below Irving, Holmes and Lowell—nay, actually below Artemus Ward, Josh Billings and Petroleum V. Nasby! The thing is fabulous, fantastic, *unglaublich*—but nevertheless true. Lacking the "higher artistic or moral purpose of the greater humourists" (*exempli gratia*, Rabelais, Molière, Aristophanes!!), Mark is dismissed by this Professor Balderdash as a hollow buffoon. . . . But stay! Do not laugh yet! Phelps himself, indignant at the stupidity, now proceeds to credit Mark with a moral purpose! . . . Turn to "The Mysterious Stranger," or "What is Man?". . .

College professors, alas, never learn anything. The identical gentleman who achieved this discovery about old Mark in 1910, now seeks to dispose of Dreiser in the exact manner of Richardson. That is to say, he essays to finish him by putting him into Coventry, by loftily passing over him. "Do not speak of him," said Kingsley of Heine; "he was a wicked man!" Search the latest volume of the Phelps revelation, "The Advance of the English Novel," and you will find that Dreiser is not once mentioned in it. The late O. Henry is hailed as a genius who will have "abiding fame"; Henry Sydnor Harrison is hymned as "more than a clever novelist," nay, "a valuable ally of the angels" (the right-thinker complex! art as a form of snuffling!), and an obscure Pagliaccio named Charles D. Stewart is brought forward as "the American novelist most worthy to fill the particular vacancy caused by the death of Mark Twain"—but Dreiser is not even listed in the index. And where Phelps leads with his baton of birch most of the other drovers of rah-rah boys follow. I turn, for example, to "An Introduction to American Literature," by Henry S. Pancoast, A.M., L.H.D., dated 1912. There are kind words for Richard Harding Davis, for Amélie Rives, and even for Will N. Harben, but not a syllable for Dreiser. Again, there is a "A History of American Literature," by Reuben Post Halleck, A.M., LL.D., dated 1911. Lew Wallace, Marietta Holley, Owen Wister and Augusta Evans Wilson have their hearings, but not Dreiser. Yet again, there is "A History of American Literature Since 1870," by Prof. Fred Lewis Pattee,[1] instructor in "the English language and literature" somewhere in Pennsylvania. Pattee has praises for Marion Crawford, Margaret Deland and F. Hopkinson Smith, and polite bows for Richard Harding Davis and Robert W. Chambers, but from end to end of his fat tome I am unable to find the slightest mention of Dreiser.

So much for one group of heroes of the new Dunciad. That it includes most of the acknowledged heavyweights of the craft—the Babbitts, Mores, Brownells and so on—goes without saying; as Van Wyck Brooks has pointed out,[2] these magnificoes are austerely above any consideration of the literature that is in being. The other group, more courageous and more honest, proceeds by direct attack; Dreiser is to be disposed of by a moral *attentat*. Its leaders are two more professors, Stuart P. Sherman and H. W. Boynton, and in its ranks march the lady critics of the newspapers, with much shrill, falsetto clamour. Sherman is the only one of them who shows any intelligible reasoning. Boynton, as always, is a mere parroter of conventional phrases, and the objections of the

1 New York, The Century Co., 1916.

2 In *The Seven Arts*, May, 1917.

ladies fade imperceptibly into a pious indignation which is indistinguishable from that of the professional suppressors of vice.

What, then, is Sherman's complaint? In brief, that Dreiser is a liar when he calls himself a realist; that he is actually a naturalist, and hence accursed. That "he has evaded the enterprise of representing human conduct, and confined himself to a representation of animal behaviour." That he "imposes his own naturalistic philosophy" upon his characters, making them do what they ought not to do, and think what they ought not to think. That "he has just two things to tell us about Frank Cowperwood: that he has a rapacious appetite for money, and a rapacious appetite for women." That this alleged "theory of animal behaviour" is not only incorrect but downright immoral, and that "when one-half the world attempts to assert it, the other half rises in battle." [1]

Only a glance is needed to show the vacuity of all this *brutum fulmen.* Dreiser, in point of fact, is scarcely more the realist or the naturalist, in any true sense, than H. G. Wells or the later George Moore, nor has he ever announced himself in either the one character or the other—if there be, in fact, any difference between them that any one save a

[1] The *Nation,* Dec. 2, 1915.

pigeon-holding pedagogue can discern. He is really something quite different, and, in his moments, something far more stately. His aim is not merely to record, but to translate and understand; the thing he exposes is not the empty event and act, but the endless mystery out of which it springs; his pictures have a passionate compassion in them that it is hard to separate from poetry. If this sense of the universal and inexplicable tragedy, if this vision of life as a seeking without a finding, if this adept summoning up of moving images, is mistaken by college professors for the empty, meticulous nastiness of Zola in "Pot-Bouille"—in Nietzsche's phrase, for "the delight to stink"—then surely the folly of college professors, as vast as it seems, has been underestimated. What is the fact? The fact is that Dreiser's attitude of mind, his manner of reaction to the phenomena he represents, the whole of his alleged "naturalistic philosophy," stems directly, not from Zola, Flaubert, Augier and the younger Dumas, but from the Greeks. In the midst of democratic cocksureness and Christian sentimentalism, of doctrinaire shallowness and professorial smugness, he stands for a point of view which at least has something honest and courageous about it; here, at all events, he is a realist. Let him put a motto to his books, and it might be:

Ἰὼ γενεαὶ βροτῶν,
Ὡς ὑμᾶς ἴσα χαὶ τὸ μηδὲν
Ζώσας ἐναριθμῶ.

If you protest against that as too harsh for Christians and college professors, right-thinkers and forward-lookers, then you protest against "Oedipus Rex." [1]

As for the animal behaviour prattle of the learned head-master, it reveals, on the one hand, only the academic fondness for seizing upon high-sounding but empty phrases and using them to alarm the populace, and on the other hand, only the academic incapacity for observing facts correctly and reporting them honestly. The truth is, of course, that the behaviour of such men as Cowperwood and Witla and of such women as Carrie and Jennie, as Dreiser describes it, is no more merely animal than the behaviour of such acknowledged and undoubted human beings as Woodrow Wilson and Jane Addams. The whole point of the story of Witla, to take the example which seems to concern the horrified watchmen most, is this: that his life is a bitter conflict between the animal in him and the aspiring soul, between the flesh and the spirit, be-

[1] 1186-1189. So translated by Floyd Dell: "O ye deathward-going tribes of man, what do your lives mean except that they go to nothingness?"

tween what is weak in him and what is strong, between what is base and what is noble. Moreover, the good, in the end, gets its hooks into the bad: as we part from Witla he is actually bathed in the tears of remorse, and resolved to be a correct and godfearing man. And what have we in "The Financier" and "The Titan"? A conflict, in the ego of Cowperwood, between aspiration and ambition, between the passion for beauty and the passion for power. Is either passion animal? To ask the question is to answer it.

I single out Dr. Sherman, not because his pompous syllogisms have any plausibility in fact or logic, but simply because he may well stand as archetype of the booming, indignant corrupter of criteria, the moralist turned critic. A glance at his paean to Arnold Bennett [1] at once reveals the true gravamen of his objection to Dreiser. What offends him is not actually Dreiser's shortcoming as an artist, but Dreiser's shortcoming as a Christian and an American. In Bennett's volumes of pseudo-philosophy—*e.g.*, "The Plain Man and His Wife" and "The Feast of St. Friend"—he finds the intellectual victuals that are to his taste. Here we have a sweet commingling of virtuous conformity and complacent optimism, of sonorous

[1] The New York *Evening Post*, Dec. 31, 1915.

platitude and easy certainty—here, in brief, we have the philosophy of the English middle classes —and here, by the same token, we have the sort of guff that the half-educated of our own country can understand. It is the calm, superior numskullery that was Victorian; it is by Samuel Smiles out of Hannah More. The offence of Dreiser is that he has disdained this revelation and gone back to the Greeks. Lo, he reads poetry into "the appetite for women"—he rejects the Pauline doctrine that all love is below the diaphragm! He thinks of Ulysses, not as a mere heretic and criminal, but as a great artist. He sees the life of man, not as a simple theorem in Calvinism, but as a vast adventure, an enchantment, a mystery. It is no wonder that respectable school-teachers are against him. . . .

The comstockian attack upon "The 'Genius'" seems to have sprung out of the same muddled sense of Dreiser's essential hostility to all that is safe and regular—of the danger in him to that mellowed Methodism which has become the national ethic. The book, in a way, was a direct challenge, for though it came to an end upon a note which even a Methodist might hear as sweet, there were undoubted provocations in detail. Dreiser, in fact, allowed his scorn to make off with his taste—and *es ist nichts fürchterlicher als Einbildungskraft ohne Geschmack.* The Comstocks arose to the bait a bit slowly, but none the less surely. Going through the volume with the terrible industry of a Sunday-school boy dredging up pearls of smut from the Old Testament, they achieved a list of no less than 89 alleged floutings of the code—75 described as lewd and 14 as profane. An inspection of these specifications affords mirth of a rare and lofty variety; nothing could more cruelly expose the inner chambers of the moral mind. When young Witla, fastening his best girl's skate, is so overcome by the carnality of youth that he hugs her, it is set down as lewd. On page 51, having become an art student, he is fired by "a great, warm-tinted nude of Bouguereau"—lewd again. On page 70 he begins to draw from the figure, and his instructor cautions him that the female breast is round, not square—more lewdness. On page 151 he kisses a girl on mouth and neck and she cautions him: "Be careful! Mamma may come in"—still more. On page 161, having got rid of mamma, she yields "herself to him gladly, joyously" and he is greatly shocked when she argues that an artist (she is by way of being a singer) had better not marry—lewdness doubly damned. On page 245 he and his bride, being ignorant, neglect the principles laid down by Dr. Sylvanus Stall in his great works on sex hygiene—lewdness most horrible! But there is no need to proceed further. Every kiss, hug and tickle of the chin in the chronicle is laboriously snouted out, empanelled, exhibited. Every hint that Witla is no vestal, that he indulges his unchristian fleshliness, that he burns in the manner of I Corinthians, VII, 9, is uncovered to the moral inquisition.

On the side of profanity there is a less ardent pursuit of evidences, chiefly, I daresay, because their unearthing is less stimulating. (Beside, there is no law prohibiting profanity in books: the whole inquiry here is but so much *lagniappe.*) On page 408, in describing a character called Daniel C. Summerfield, Dreiser says that the fellow is "very much given to swearing, more as a matter of habit than of foul intention," and then goes on to explain somewhat lamely that "no picture of him would be complete without the interpolation of his various expressions." They turn out to be *God damn* and *Jesus Christ*—three of the latter and five or six of the former. All go down; the pure in heart must be shielded from the knowledge of them. (But what of the immoral French? They call the English *Goddams.*) Also, three plain *damns,* eight *hells*, one *my God*, five *by Gods*, one *go to the devil*, one *God Almighty* and one plain *God*. Altogether, 31 specimens are listed. "The 'Genius'" runs to 350,000 words. The profanity thus works out to somewhat less than one word in 10,000. . . . Alas, the comstockian proboscis, feeling for such offendings, is not as alert as when uncovering more savoury delicacies. On page 191 I find an overlooked *by God*. On page 372 there are *Oh God, God curse her*, and *God strike her dead*. On page 373 there are *Ah God, Oh God* and three other invocations of God. On page 617 there is *God help me*. On page 720 there is *as God is my judge*. On page 723 there is *I'm no damned good*. . . . But I begin to blush.

When the Comstock Society began proceedings against "The 'Genius,'" a group of English novelists, including Arnold Bennett, H. G. Wells, W. L. George and Hugh Walpole, cabled an indignant caveat. This bestirred the Author's League of America to activity, and its executive committee issued a minute denouncing the business. Later on a protest of American *literati* was circulated, and more than 400 signed, including such highly respectable authors as Winston Churchill, Percy MacKaye, Booth Tarkington and James Lane Allen, and such critics as Lawrence Gilman, Clayton

Hamilton and James Huneker, and the editors of such journals as the *Century*, the *Atlantic Monthly* and the *New Republic.* Among my literary lumber is all the correspondence relating to this protest, not forgetting the letters of those who refused to sign, and some day I hope to publish it, that posterity may not lose the joy of an extremely diverting episode. The case attracted wide attention and was the theme of an extraordinarily violent discussion, but the resultant benefits to Dreiser were more than counterbalanced, I daresay, by the withdrawal of "The 'Genius'" itself.[1]

§ 7

Dreiser, like Mark Twain and Emerson before him, has been far more hospitably greeted in his first stage, now drawing to a close, in England than in his own country. The cause of this, I daresay, lies partly in the fact that "Sister Carrie" was in general circulation over there during the seven years that it remained suppressed on this side. It was during these years that such men as Arnold Bennett, Theodore Watts-Dunton, Frank Harris and

1 Despite the comstockian attack, Dreiser is still fairly well represented on the shelves of American public libraries. A canvas of the libraries of the 25 principal cities gives the following result, an × indicating that the corresponding book is catalogued, and a — that is not: [Over]

H. G. Wells, and such critical journals as the *Spectator,* the *Saturday Review* and the *Athenaeum* be-

	Sister Carrie	Jennie Gerhardt	The Financier	The Titan	A Traveler at Forty	The "Genius"	Plays of the Natural	A Hoosier Holiday
New York	×	—	—	×	×	×	×	×
Boston	—	—	—	—	×	—	×	—
Chicago	×	×	×	×	×	×	×	×
Philadelphia	×	×	×	×	×	×	×	×
Washington	—	—	—	—	×	—	×	—
Baltimore	—	—	—	—	×	—	—	—
Pittsburgh	—	—	×	×	×	×	—	×
New Orleans	—	—	—	—	—	—	—	—
Denver	×	×	×	×	×	×	×	×
San Francisco	×	×	×	×	×	—	—	×
St. Louis	×	×	×	×	×	—	×	—
Cleveland	×	×	×	×	—	×	×	—
Providence	—	—	—	—	—	—	—	—
Los Angeles	×	×	×	×	×	×	×	×
Indianapolis	×	×	×	—	×	—	×	×
Louisville	×	×	—	×	×	×	×	×
St. Paul	×	×	—	—	×	—	×	×
Minneapolis	×	×	×	—	×	—	×	—
Cincinnati	×	×	×	—	×	—	×	×
Kansas City	×	×	×	×	×	×	×	×
Milwaukee	—	—	—	—	×	—	×	×
Newark	×	×	×	×	×	×	×	×
Detroit	×	×	×	—	×	×	×	×
Seattle	×	×	—	—	×	—	×	×
Hartford	—	—	—	—	—	—	—	×

[Over]

came aware of him, and so laid the foundations of a sound appreciation of his subsequent work. Since the beginning of the war, certain English newspapers have echoed the alarmed American discovery that he is a literary agent of the Wilhelmstrasse, but it is to the honour of the English that this imbecility has got no countenance from reputable authority and has not injured his position.

At home, as I have shown, he is less fortunate. When criticism is not merely an absurd effort to chase him out of court because his ideas are not orthodox, as the Victorians tried to chase out Darwin and Swinburne, and their predecessors pursued Shelley and Byron, it is too often designed to identify him with some branch or other of "radical" poppycock, and so credit him with purposes he has never imagined. Thus Chautauqua pulls and Greenwich Village pushes. In the middle

This table shows that but two libraries, those of Providence and New Orleans, bar Dreiser altogether. The effect of alarms from newspaper reviewers is indicated by the scant distribution of the The "Genius," which is barred by 14 of the 25. It should be noted that some of these libraries issue certain of the books only under restrictions. This I know to be the case in Louisville, Los Angeles, Newark and Cleveland. The Newark librarian informs me that Jennie Gerhardt is to be removed altogether, presumably in response to some protest from local Comstocks. In Chicago The "Genius" has been stolen, and on account of the withdrawal of the book the Public Library has been unable to get another copy.

ground there proceeds the pedantic effort to dispose of him by labelling him. One faction maintains that he is a realist; another calls him a naturalist; a third argues that he is really a disguised romanticist. This debate is all sound and fury, signifying nothing, but out of it has come a valuation by Lawrence Gilman [1] which perhaps strikes very close to the truth. He is, says Mr. Gilman, "a sentimental mystic who employs the mimetic gestures of the realist." This judgment is apt in particular and sound in general. No such thing as a pure method is possible in the novel. Plain realism, as in Gorky's "Nachtasyl" and the war stories of Ambrose Bierce, simply wearies us by its vacuity; plain romance, if we ever get beyond our nonage, makes us laugh. It is their artistic combination, as in life itself, that fetches us—the subtle projection of the concrete muddle that is living against the ideal orderliness that we reach out for—the eternal war of experience and aspiration—the contrast between the world as it is and the world as it might be or ought to be. Dreiser describes the thing that he sees, laboriously and relentlessly, but he never forgets the dream that is behind it. "He gives you," continues Mr. Gilman, "a sense of actuality; but he gives you more than

[1] The *North American Review*, Feb., 1916.

that: out of the vast welter and surge, the plethoric irrelevancies, . . . emerges a sense of the infinite sadness and mystery of human life." . . .[1]

"To see truly," said Renan, "is to see dimly." Dimness or mystery, call it what you will: it is in all these overgrown and formless, but profoundly moving books. Just what do they mean? Just what is Dreiser driving at? That such questions should be asked is only a proof of the straits to which pedagogy has brought criticism. The answer is simple: he is driving at nothing, he is merely trying to represent what he sees and feels. His moving impulse is no flabby yearning to teach, to expound, to make simple; it is that "obscure inner necessity" of which Conrad tells us, the irresistible creative passion of a genuine artist, standing spell-bound before the impenetrable enigma that is life, enamoured by the strange beauty that plays over its sordidness, challenged to a wondering and half-terrified sort of representation of what passes understanding. And *jenseits von Gut und Böse*. "For myself," says Dreiser, "I do not know what truth is, what beauty is, what love is, what hope is. I do not believe any one absolutely and I do not doubt any one absolutely. I think peo-

[1] Another competent valuation, by Randolph Bourne, is in *The Dial*, June 14, 1917.

ple are both evil and well-intentioned." The hatching of the Dreiser bugaboo is here; it is the flat rejection of the rubber-stamp formulae that outrages petty minds; not being "good," he must be "evil"—as William Blake said of Milton, a true poet is always "of the devil's party." But in that very groping toward a light but dimly seen there is a measure, it seems to me, of Dreiser's rank and consideration as an artist. "Now comes the public," says Hermann Bahr, "and demands that we explain what the poet is trying to say. The answer is this: If we knew exactly he would not be a poet. . . ."

III. JAMES HUNEKER

III

JAMES HUNEKER

§ 1

EDGAR ALLAN POE, I am fond of believing, earned as a critic a good deal of the excess of praise that he gets as a romancer and a poet, and another over-estimated American dithyrambist, Sidney Lanier, wrote the best text-book of prosody in English; [1] but in general the critical writing done in the United States has been of a low order, and most American writers of any genuine distinction, like most American painters and musicians, have had to wait for understanding until it appeared abroad. The case of Emerson is typical. At thirty, he was known in New England as a heretical young clergyman and no more, and his fame threatened to halt at the tea-tables of the Boston Brahmins. It remained for Landor and Carlyle, in a strange land, to discern his higher potentialities, and to encourage him to his real life-work. Mark Twain, as I have hitherto shown, suf-

1 The Science of English Verse; New York, Scribner, 1880.

fered from the same lack of critical perception at home. He was quickly recognized as a funny fellow, true enough, but his actual stature was not even faintly apprehended, and even after "Huckleberry Finn" he was still bracketed with such laborious farceurs as Artemus Ward. It was Sir Walter Besant, an Englishman, who first ventured to put him on his right shelf, along with Swift, Cervantes and Molière. As for Poe and Whitman, the native recognition of their genius was so greatly conditioned by a characteristic horror of their immorality that it would be absurd to say that their own country understood them. Both were better and more quickly apprehended in France, and it was in France, not in America, that each founded a school. What they had to teach we have since got back at second hand—the tale of mystery, which was Poe's contribution, through Gaboriau and Boisgobey; and *vers libre,* which was Whitman's, through the French *imagistes.*

The cause of this profound and almost unbroken lack of critical insight and enterprise, this puerile Philistinism and distrust of ideas among us, is partly to be found, it seems to me, in the fact that the typical American critic is quite without any adequate cultural equipment for the office he presumes to fill. Dr. John Dewey, in some late remarks upon the American universities, has perhaps shown the cause thereof. The trouble with our educational method, he argues, is that it falls between the two stools of English humanism and German relentlessness—that it produces neither a man who intelligently feels nor a man who thoroughly knows. Criticism, in America, is a function of this half-educated and conceited class; it is not a popular art, but an esoteric one; even in its crassest journalistic manifestations it presumes to a certain academic remoteness from the concerns and carnalities of everyday. In every aspect it shows the defects of its practitioners. The American critic of beautiful letters, in his common incarnation, is no more than a talented sophomore, or, at best, a somewhat absurd professor. He suffers from a palpable lack of solid preparation; he has no background of moving and illuminating experience behind him; his soul has not sufficiently adventured among masterpieces, nor among men. Imagine a Taine or a Sainte-Beuve or a Macaulay —man of the world, veteran of philosophies, "lord of life"—and you imagine his complete antithesis. Even on the side of mere professional knowledge, the primary material of his craft, he always appears incompletely outfitted. The grand sweep and direction of the literary currents elude him;

he is eternally on the surface, chasing bits of driftwood. The literature he knows is the fossil literature taught in colleges—worse, in high schools. It must be dead before he is aware of it. And in particular he appears ignorant of what is going forward in other lands. An exotic idea, to penetrate his consciousness, must first become stale, and even then he is apt to purge it of all its remaining validity and significance before adopting it.

This has been true since the earliest days. Emerson himself, though a man of unusual discernment and a diligent drinker from German spigots, nevertheless remained a *dilettante* in both aesthetics and metaphysics to the end of his days, and the incompleteness of his equipment never showed more plainly than in his criticism of books. Lowell, if anything, was even worse; his aesthetic theory, first and last, was nebulous and superficial, and all that remains of his pleasant essays today is their somewhat smoky pleasantness. He was a Charles Dudley Warner in nobler trappings, but still, at bottom, a Charles Dudley Warner. As for Poe, though he was by nature a far more original and penetrating critic than either Emerson or Lowell, he was enormously ignorant of good books, and moreover, he could never quite throw off a congenital vulgarity of taste, so painfully visible in the strutting of his style. The man, for all his grand dreams, had a shoddy soul; he belonged authentically to the era of cuspidors, "females" and Sons of Temperance. His occasional affectation of scholarship has deceived no one. It was no more than Yankee bluster; he constantly referred to books that he had never read. Beside, the typical American critic of those days was not Poe, but his arch-enemy, Rufus Wilmot Griswold, that almost fabulous ass—a Baptist preacher turned taster of the beautiful. Imagine a Baptist valuing Balzac, or Molière, or Shakespeare, or Goethe—or Rabelais!

Coming down to our own time, one finds the same endless amateurishness, so characteristic of everything American, from politics to cookery—the same astounding lack of training and vocation. Consider the solemn ponderosities of the pious old maids, male and female, who write book reviews for the newspapers. Here we have a heavy pretension to culture, a campus cocksureness, a laborious righteousness—but of sound aesthetic understanding, of alertness and hospitality to ideas, not a trace. The normal American book reviewer, indeed, is an elderly virgin, a superstitious bluestocking, an apostle of Vassar *Kultur;* and her customary attitude of mind is one of fascinated horror. (The Hamilton Wright Mabie complex! The "white list" of novels!) William Dean Howells, despite a certain jauntiness and even kittenishness of manner, was spiritually of that company. For all his phosphorescent heresies, he was what the uplifters call a right-thinker at heart, and soaked in the national tradition. He was easiest intrigued, not by force and originality, but by a sickly, *Ladies' Home Journal* sort of piquancy; it was this that made him see a genius in the Philadelphia Zola, W. B. Trites, and that led him to hymn an abusive business letter by Frank A. Munsey, author of "The Boy Broker" and "Afloat in a Great City," as a significant human document. Moreover Howells ran true to type in another way, for he long reigned as the leading Anglo-Saxon authority on the Russian novelists without knowing, so far as I can make out, more than ten words of Russian. In the same manner, we have had enthusiasts for D'Annunzio and Mathilde Serao who knew no Italian, and celebrants of Maeterlinck and Verhaeren whose French was of the finishing school, and Ibsen authorities without a single word of Dano-Norwegian—I met one once who failed to recognize "Et Dukkehjem" as the original title of "A Doll's House,"—and performers upon Hauptmann who could no more read "Die Weber" than they could decipher a tablet of Tiglath-Pileser III.

Here and there, of course, a more competent critic of beautiful letters flings out his banner—for example, John Macy, Ludwig Lewisohn, André Tridon, Francis Hackett, Van Wyck Brooks, Burton Rascoe, E. A. Boyd, Llewellyn Jones, Otto Heller, J. E. Spingarn, Lawrence Gilman, the late J. Percival Pollard. Well-informed, intelligent, wide-eyed men—but only four of them even Americans, and not one of them with a wide audience, or any appreciable influence upon the main stream of American criticism. Pollard's best work is buried in the perfumed pages of *Town Topics;* his book on the Munich wits and dramatists [1] is almost unknown. Heller and Lewisohn make their way slowly; a patriotic wariness, I daresay, mixes itself up with their acceptance. Gilman disperses his talents; he is quite as much musician as critic of the arts. As for Macy, I recently found his "The Spirit of American Literature," [2] by long odds the soundest, wisest book on its subject, selling for fifty cents on a Fifth avenue remainder counter.

How many remain? A few competent reviewers who are primarily something else—Harvey,

[1] Masks and Minstrels of New Germany; Boston, John W. Luce & Co., 1911.

[2] New York, Doubleday, Page & Co., 1913.

Aikin, Untermeyer and company. A few youngsters on the newspapers, struggling against the business office. And then a leap to the Victorians, the crêpe-clad pundits, the bombastic word-mongers of the campus school—H. W. Boynton, W. C. Brownell, Paul Elmer More, William Lyon Phelps, Frederick Taber Cooper *et al.* Here, undoubtedly, we have learning of a sort. More, it appears, once taught Sanskrit to the adolescent suffragettes of Bryn Mawr—an enterprise as stimulating (and as intelligible) as that of setting off fire-works in a blind asylum. Phelps sits in a chair at Yale. Boynton is a master of arts in English literature, whatever that may mean. Brownell is both L.H.D. and Litt.D., thus surpassing Samuel Johnson by one point, and Hazlitt, Coleridge and Malone by two. But the learning of these august *umbilicarii*, for all its pretensions, is precisely the sterile, foppish sort one looks for in second-rate college professors. The appearance is there, but not the substance. One ingests a horse-doctor's dose of words, but fails to acquire any illumination. Read More on Nietzsche [1] if you want to find out just how stupid criticism can be, and yet show the outward forms of sense. Read Phelps'

[1] The Drift of Romanticism; Boston, Houghton Mifflin Co., 1913.

"The Advance of the English Novel"[1] if you would see a fine art treated as a moral matter, and great works tested by the criteria of a small-town Sunday-school, and all sorts of childish sentimentality whooped up. And plough through Brownell's "Standards,"[2] if you have the patience, and then try to reduce its sonorous platitudes to straightforward and defensible propositions.

§ 2

Now for the exception. He is, of course, James Gibbons Huneker, the solitary Iokanaan in this tragic aesthetic wilderness, the only critic among us whose vision sweeps the whole field of beauty, and whose reports of what he sees there show any genuine gusto. That gusto of his, I fancy, is two-thirds of his story. It is unquenchable, contagious, inflammatory; he is the only performer in the commissioned troupe who knows how to arouse his audience to anything approaching enthusiasm. The rest, even including Howells, are pedants lecturing to the pure in heart, but Huneker makes a joyous story of it; his exposition, transcending the merely expository, takes on the quality of an ad-

[1] New York, Dodd, Mead & Co., 1916.
[2] New York, Chas. Scribner's Sons, 1917.

venture hospitably shared. One feels, reading him, that he is charmed by the men and women he writes about, and that their ideas, even when he rejects them, give him an agreeable stimulation. And to the charm that he thus finds and exhibits in others, he adds the very positive charm of his own personality. He seems a man who has found the world fascinating, if perhaps not perfect; a friendly and good-humoured fellow; no frigid scholiast, but something of an epicure; in brief, the reverse of the customary maker of books about books. Compare his two essays on Ibsen, in "Egoists" and "Iconoclasts," to the general body of American writing upon the great Norwegian. The difference is that between a portrait and a Bertillon photograph, Richard Strauss and Czerny, a wedding and an autopsy. Huneker displays Ibsen, not as a petty mystifier of the women's clubs, but as a literary artist of large skill and exalted passion, and withal a quite human and understandable man. These essays were written at the height of the symbolism madness; in their own way, they even show some reflection of it; but taking them in their entirety, how clearly they stand above the ignorant obscurantism of the prevailing criticism of the time—how immeasurably superior they are, for example, to that favourite hymn-book of the

Ibsenites, "The Ibsen Secret" by Jennette Lee! For the causes of this difference one need not seek far. They are to be found in the difference between the bombastic half-knowledge of a school teacher and the discreet and complete knowledge of a man of culture. Huneker is that man of culture. He has reported more of interest and value than any other American critic, living or dead, but the essence of his criticism does not lie so much in what he specifically reports as in the civilized point of view from which he reports it. He is a true cosmopolitan, not only in the actual range of his adventurings, but also and more especially in his attitude of mind. His world is not America, nor Europe, nor Christendom, but the whole universe of beauty. As Jules Simon said of Taine: "*Aucun écrivain de nos jours n'a . . . découvert plus d'horizons variés et immenses.*"

Need anything else be said in praise of a critic? And does an extravagance or an error here and there lie validly against the saying of it? I think not. I could be a professor if I would and show you slips enough—certain ponderous nothings in the Ibsen essays, already mentioned; a too easy bemusement at the hands of Shaw; a vacillating over Wagner; a habit of yielding to the hocus-pocus of the mystics, particularly Maeterlinck.

On the side of painting, I am told, there are even worse aberrations; I know too little about painting to judge for myself. But the list, made complete, would still not be over-long, and few of its items would be important. Huneker, like the rest of us, has sinned his sins, but his judgments, in the overwhelming main, hold water. He has resisted the lure of all the wild movements of the generation; the tornadoes of doctrine have never knocked him over. Nine times out of ten, in estimating a new man in music or letters, he has come curiously close to the truth at the first attempt. And he has always announced it in good time; his solo has always preceded the chorus. He was, I believe, the first American (not forgetting William Morton Payne and Hjalmar Hjorth Boyesen, the pioneers) to write about Ibsen with any understanding of the artist behind the prophet's mask; he was the first to see the rising star of Nietzsche (this was back in 1888); he was beating a drum for Shaw the critic before ever Shaw the dramatist and mob philosopher was born (*circa* 1886–1890); he was writing about Hauptmann and Maeterlinck before they had got well set on their legs in their own countries; his estimate of Sudermann, bearing date of 1905, may stand with scarcely the change of a word today; he did a lot of valiant pioneering for Strindberg, Hervieu, Stirner and Gorki, and later on helped in the pioneering for Conrad; he was in the van of the MacDowell enthusiasts; he fought for the ideas of such painters as Davies, Lawson, Luks, Sloan and Prendergest (Americans all, by the way: an answer to the hollow charge of exotic obsession) at a time when even Manet, Monet and Degas were laughed at; he was among the first to give a hand to Frank Norris, Theodore Dreiser, Stephen Crane and H. B. Fuller. In sum, he gave some semblance of reality in the United States, after other men had tried and failed, to that great but ill-starred revolt against Victorian pedantry, formalism and sentimentality which began in the early 90's. It would be difficult, indeed, to overestimate the practical value to all the arts in America of his intellectual alertness, his catholic hospitality to ideas, his artistic courage, and above all, his powers of persuasion. It was not alone that he saw clearly what was sound and significant; it was that he managed, by the sheer charm of his writings, to make a few others see and understand it. If the United States is in any sort of contact today, however remotely, with what is aesthetically going on in the more civilized countries—if the Puritan tradition, for all its firm entrenchment, has eager and resourceful enemies besetting it—if the pall of Harvard quasi-culture, by the Oxford manner out of Calvinism, has been lifted ever so little—there is surely no man who can claim a larger share of credit for preparing the way. . . .

§ 3

Huneker comes out of Philadelphia, that depressing intellectual slum, and his first writing was for the Philadelphia *Evening Bulletin.* He is purely Irish in blood, and is of very respectable ancestry, his maternal grandfather and godfather having been James Gibbons, the Irish poet and patriot, and president of the Fenian Brotherhood in America. Once, in a review of "The Pathos of Distance," I ventured the guess that there was a German strain in him somewhere, and based it upon the beery melancholy visible in parts of that book. Who but a German sheds tears over the empty bottles of day before yesterday, the Adelaide Neilson of 1877? Who but a German goes into woollen undershirts at 45, and makes his will, and begins to call his wife "Mamma"? The green-sickness of youth is endemic from pole to pole, as much so as measles; but what race save the wicked one is floored by a blue distemper in middle age, with sentimental burblings *a cappella,* hallucinations of lost loves, and an unquenchable lacrymorrhea? . . . I made out a good case, but I was wrong, and the penalty came swiftly and doubly, for on the one hand the Boston *Transcript* sounded an alarm against both Huneker and me as German spies, and on the other hand Huneker himself proclaimed that, even spiritually, he was less German than Magyar, less "Hun" than Hun. "I am," he said, "a Celto-Magyar: Pilsner at Donneybrook Fair. Even the German beer and cuisine are not in it with the Austro-Hungarian." Here, I suspect, he meant to say Czech instead of Magyar, for isn't Pilsen in Bohemia? Moreover, turn to the chapter on Prague in "New Cosmopolis," and you will find out in what highland his heart really is. In this book, indeed, is a vast hymn to all things Czechic—the Pilsen *Urquell,* the muffins stuffed with poppy-seed jam, the spiced chicken liver *en casserole,* the pretty Bohemian girls, the rose and golden glory of Hradschin Hill. . . . One thinks of other strange infatuations: the Polish Conrad's for England, the Scotch Mackay's for Germany, the Low German Brahms' for Italy. Huneker, I daresay, is the first Celto-Czech—or Celto-Magyar, as you choose. (Maybe the name suggests something. It is not to be debased to *Hoon*-eker, remember, but kept at *Hun*-eker, rhyming initially with *nun* and *gun.*)

An unearthly marriage of elements, by all the gods! but there are pretty children of it. . . .

Philadelphia humanely disgorged Huneker in 1878. His father designed him for the law, and he studied the institutes at the Philadelphia Law Academy, but like Schumann, he was spoiled for briefs by the stronger pull of music and the *cacoëthes scribendi.* (Grandpa John Huneker had been a composer of church music, and organist at St. Mary's.) In the year mentioned he set out for Paris to see Liszt; his aim was to make himself a piano virtuoso. His name does not appear on his own exhaustive list of Liszt pupils, but he managed to quaff of the Pierian spring at second-hand, for he had lessons from Theodore Ritter (*né* Bennet), a genuine pupil of the old walrus, and he was also taught by the venerable Georges Mathias, a pupil of Chopin. These days laid the foundations for two subsequent books, the "Chopin: the Man and His Music" of 1900, and the "Franz Liszt" of 1911. More, they prepared the excavations for all of the others, for Huneker began sending home letters to the Philadelphia *Bulletin* on the pictures that he saw, the books that he read and the music that he heard in Paris, and out of them gradually grew a body of doctrine that was to be developed into full-length criticism on his return to the United States. He stayed in Paris until the middle 80's, and then settled in New York.

All the while his piano studies continued, and in New York he became a pupil of Rafael Joseffy. He even became a teacher himself and was for ten years on the staff of the National Conservatory, and showed himself at all the annual meetings of the Music Teachers' Association. But bit by bit criticism elbowed out music-making, as music-making had elbowed out criticism with Schumann and Berlioz. In 1886 or thereabout he joined the *Musical Courier;* then he went, in succession, to the old *Recorder,* to the *Morning Advertiser,* to the *Sun,* to the *Times,* and finally to the Philadelphia *Press* and the New York *World.* Various weeklies and monthlies have also enlisted him: *Mlle. New York,* the *Atlantic Monthly,* the *Smart Set,* the *North American Review* and *Scribner's.* He has even stooped to *Puck,* vainly trying to make an American *Simplicissimus* of that dull offspring of synagogue and barbershop. He has been, in brief, an extremely busy and not too fastidious journalist, writing first about one of the arts, and then about another, and then about all seven together. But music has been the steadiest of all his loves; his first three books dealt almost wholly with it; of his complete canon more than half have to do with it.

§ 4

His first book, "Mezzotints in Modern Music," published in 1899, revealed his predilections clearly, and what is more, his critical insight and sagacity. One reads it today without the slightest feeling that it is an old story; some of the chapters, obviously reworkings of articles for the papers, must go back to the middle 90's, and yet the judgments they proclaim scarcely call for the change of a word. The single noticeable weakness is a too easy acquiescence in the empty showiness of Saint-Saëns, a tendency to bow to the celebrated French parlour magician too often. Here, I dare say, is an echo of old Paris days, for Camille was a hero on the Seine in 1880, and there was even talk of pitting him against Wagner. The estimates of other men are judiciously arrived at and persuasively stated. Tschaikowsky is correctly put down as a highly talented but essentially shallow fellow—a blubberer in the regalia of a philosopher. Brahms, then still under attack by Henry T. Finck, of the *Evening Post* (the press-agent of Massenet:

ye gods, what Harvard can do, even to a Würtemberger!) is subjected to a long, an intelligent and an extremely friendly analysis; no better has got into English since, despite too much stress on the piano music. And Richard Strauss, yet a nine days' wonder, is described clearly and accurately, and his true stature indicated. The rest of the book is less noteworthy; Huneker says the proper things about Chopin, Liszt and Wagner, and adds a chapter on piano methods, the plain fruit of his late pedagogy. But the three chapters I have mentioned are enough; they fell, in their time, into a desert of stupidity; they set a standard in musical criticism in America that only Huneker himself has ever exceeded.

The most popular of his music books, of course, is the "Chopin" (1900). Next to "Iconoclasts," it is the best seller of them all. More, it has been done into German, French and Italian, and is chiefly responsible for Huneker's celebrity abroad as the only critic of music that America has ever produced. Superficially, it seems to be a monument of pedantry, a meticulous piling up of learning, but a study of it shows that it is very much more than that. Compare it to Sir George Grove's staggering tome on the Beethoven symphonies if you want to understand the difference between mere scholastic diligence and authentic criticism. The one is simply a top-heavy mass of disorderly facts and worshipping enthusiasm; the other is an analysis that searches out every nook and corner of the subject, and brings it into coherence and intelligibility. The Chopin rhapsodist is always held in check by the sound musician; there is a snouting into dark places as well as a touching up of high lights. I myself am surely no disciple of the Polish tuberose—his sweetness, in fact, gags me, and I turn even to Moszkowski for relief—but I have read and re-read this volume with endless interest, and I find it more bethumbed than any other Huneker book in my library, saving only "Iconoclasts" and "Old Fogy." Here, indeed, Huneker is on his own ground. One often feels, in his discussions of orchestral music, that he only thinks orchestrally, like Schumann, with an effort —that all music, in his mind, gets itself translated into terms of piano music. In dealing with Chopin no such transvaluation of values is necessary; the raw materials are ready for his uses without preparation; he is wholly at home among the black keys and white.

His "Liszt" is a far less noteworthy book. It is, in truth, scarcely a book at all, but merely a collection of notes for a book, some of them considerably elaborated, but others set down in the altogether. One reads it because it is about Liszt, the most fantastic figure that ever came out of Hungary, half devil and half clown; not because there is any conflagration of ideas in it. The chapter that reveals most of Huneker is the appendix on latter-day piano virtuosi, with its estimates of such men as de Pachmann, Rosenthal, Paderewski and Hofmann. Much better stuff is to be found in "Overtones," "The Pathos of Distance" and "Ivory, Apes and Peacocks"—brilliant, if not always profound studies of Strauss, Wagner, Schoenberg, Moussorgsky, and even Verdi. But if I had my choice of the whole shelf, it would rest, barring the "Chopin," on "Old Fogy"—the *scherzo* of the Hunekeran symphony, the critic taking a holiday, the Devil's Mass in the tonal sanctuary. In it Huneker is at his very choicest, making high-jinks with his Davidsbund of one, rattling the skeletons in all the musical closets of the world. Here, throwing off his critic's black gown, his lays about him right and left, knocking the reigning idols off their perches; resurrecting the old, old dead and trying to pump the breath into them; lambasting on one page and lauding on the next; lampooning his fellow critics and burlesquing their rubber stamp fustian; extolling Dussek and damning Wagner; swearing mighty oaths by Mozart, and after him, Strauss—not Richard, but Johann! The Old Fogy, of course, is the thinnest of disguises, a mere veil of gossamer for "Editor" Huneker. That Huneker in false whiskers is inimitable, incomparable, almost indescribable. On the one hand, he is a prodigy of learning, a veritable warehouse of musical information, true, half-true and apocryphal; on the other hand, he is a jester who delights in reducing all learning to absurdity. Reading him somehow suggests hearing a Bach mass rescored for two fifes, a tambourine in B, a wind machine, two tenor harps, a contrabass oboe, two banjos, eight tubas and the usual clergy and strings. The substance is there; every note is struck exactly in the middle—but what outlandish tone colours, what strange, unearthly sounds! It is not Bach, however, who first comes to mind when Huneker is at his tricks, but Papa Haydn—the Haydn of the Surprise symphony and the Farewell. There is the same gargantuan gaiety, the same magnificent irreverence. Haydn did more for the symphony than any other man, but he also got more fun out of it than any other man.

"Old Fogy," of course, is not to be taken seriously: it is frankly a piece of fooling. But all the same a serious idea runs through the book from end to end, and that is the idea that music is getting too subjective to be comfortable. The makers of symphonies tend to forget beauty altogether; their one effort is to put all their own petty trials and tribulations, their empty theories and speculations into cacophony. Even so far back as Beethoven's day that autobiographical habit had begun. "Beethoven," says Old Fogy, is "dramatic, powerful, a maker of storms, a subduer of tempests; but his speech is the speech of a self-centred egotist. He is the father of all the modern melomaniacs, who, looking into their own souls, write what they see therein—misery, corruption, slighting selfishness and ugliness." Old Ludwig's groans, of course, we can stand. He was not only a great musician, but also a great man. It is just as interesting to hear him sigh and complain as it would be to hear the private prayers of Julius Caesar. But what of Tschaikowsky, with his childish Slavic whining? What of Liszt, with his cheap playacting, his incurable lasciviousness, his plebeian warts? What of Wagner, with his delight in imbecile fables, his popinjay vanity, his soul of a *Schnorrer?* What of Richard Strauss, with his warmed-over Nietzscheism, his flair for the merely horrible? Old Fogy sweeps them all into his ragbag. If art is to be defined as beauty seen through a temperament, then give us more beauty and cleaner temperaments! Back to the old gods, Mozart and Bach, with a polite bow to Brahms and a sentimental tear for Chopin! Beethoven tried to tell his troubles in his music; Mozart was content to ravish the angels of their harps. And as for Johann Sebastian, "there was more real musical feeling, uplifting and sincerity in the old Thomaskirche in Leipzig . . . than in all your modern symphony and oratorio machine-made concerts put together."

All this is argued, to be sure, in extravagant terms. Wagner is a mere ghoul and impostor: "The Flying Dutchman" is no more than a parody on Weber, and "Parsifal" is "an outrage against religion, morals and music." Daddy Liszt is "the inventor of the Liszt pupil, a bad piano player, a venerable man with a purple nose—a Cyrano de Cognac nose." Tschaikowsky is the Slav gone crazy on vodka. He transformed Hamlet into "a yelling man" and Romeo and Juliet into "two monstrous Cossacks, who gibber and squeak at each other while reading some obscene volume." "His Manfred is a libel on Byron, who was a libel on God." And even Schumann is a vanishing star, a literary man turned composer, a pathological case. But, as I have said, a serious idea runs through all this concerto for slapstick and seltzer siphon, and to me, at least, that idea has a plentiful reasonableness. We are getting too much melodrama, too much vivisection, too much rebellion—and too little music. Turn from Tschaikowsky's Pathétique or from any of his wailing tone-poems to Schubert's C major, or to Mozart's Jupiter, or to Beethoven's *kleine Sinfonie in F dur*: it is like coming out of a *Kaffeeklatsch* into the open air, almost like escaping from a lunatic asylum. The one unmistakable emotion that much of this modern music from the steppes and morgues and *Biertische* engenders is a longing for form, clarity, coherence, a self-respecting tune. The snorts and moans of the pothouse Werthers are as irritating, in the long run, as the bawling of a child, the squeak of a pig under a gate. One yearns unspeakably for a composer who gives out his pair of honest themes, and then develops them with both ears open, and then recapitulates them unashamed, and then hangs a brisk coda to them, and then shuts up.

§ 5

So much for "Old Fogy" and the musical books. They constitute, not only the best body of work that Huneker himself has done, but the best body of musical criticism that any American has done. Musical criticism, in our great Calvinist republic, confines itself almost entirely to transient reviewing, and even when it gets between covers, it keeps its trivial quality. Consider, for example, the published work of Henry Edward Krehbiel, for long the *doyen* of the New York critics. I pick up his latest book, "A Second Book of Operas,"[1] open it at random, and find this:

> On January 31, 1893, the Philadelphia singers, aided by the New York Symphony Society, gave a performance of the opera, under the auspices of the Young Men's Hebrew Association, for the benefit of its charities, at the Carnegie Music Hall, New York. Mr. Walter Damrosch was to have conducted, but was detained in Washington by the funeral of Mr. Blaine, and Mr. Hinrichs took his place.

O Doctor *admirabilis, acutus et illuminatissimus!* Needless to say the universities have not overlooked this geyser of buttermilk: he is an honourary A.M. of Yale. His most respectable volume, that on negro folksong, impresses one principally by its incompleteness. It may be praised as a sketch, but surely not as a book. The trouble with Krehbiel, of course, is that he mistakes a newspaper morgue for Parnassus. He has all of the third-rate German's capacity for unearthing

[1] New York, The Macmillan Co., 1917.

facts, but he doesn't know how either to think or to write, and so his criticism is mere pretence and pishposh. W. J. Henderson, of the *Sun,* doesn't carry that handicap. He is as full of learning as Krehbiel, as his books on singing and on the early Italian opera show, but he also wields a slippery and intriguing pen, and he could be hugely entertaining if he would. Instead, he devotes himself to manufacturing primers for the newly intellectual. I can find little of the charm of his *Sun* articles in his books. Lawrence Gilman? A sound musician but one who of late years has often neglected music for the other arts. Philip H. Goepp? His three volumes on the symphonic repertoire leave twice as much to be said as they say. Carl Van Vechten? A very promising novice, but not yet at full growth. Philip Hale? His gigantic annotations scarcely belong to criticism at all; they are musical talmudism. Beside, they are buried in the program books of the Boston Symphony Orchestra, and might as well be inscribed on the temple walls of Baalbec. As for Upton and other such fellows, they are merely musical chautauquans, and their tedious commentaries have little more value than the literary criticisms in the religious weeklies. One of them, a Harvard *maestro,* has published a book on the orchestra in which, on separate pages, the reader is solemnly presented with pictures of first and second violins!

It seems to me that Huneker stands on a higher level than any of these industrious gentlemen, and that his writings on music are of much more value, despite his divided allegiance among the *beaux arts*. Whatever may be said against him, it must at least be admitted that he knows Chopin, and that he has written the best volumes upon the tuberculous Pole in English. Vladimir de Pachmann, that king of all Chopin players, once bore characteristic testimony to the fact—I think it was in London. The program was heavy with the études and ballades, and Huneker sat in the front row of fanatics. After a storm of applause de Pachmann rose from the piano stool, levelled a bony claw at Huneker, and pronounced his dictum: "*He* knows more than *all* of you." Joseffy seems to have had the same opinion, for he sought the aid of his old pupil in preparing his new edition of Chopin, the first volume of which is all he lived to see in print. . . . And, beyond all the others, Huneker disdains writing for the kindergarten. There is no stooping in his discourse; he frankly addresses himself to an audience that has gone through the forms, and so he avoids the tediousness of the A B C expositors. He is the only American musical critic, save Van Vechten, who thus assumes invariably that a musical audience exists, and the only one who constantly measures up to its probable interests, supposing it to be there. Such a book as "Old Fogy," for all its buffoonery, is conceivable only as the work of a sound musician. Its background is one of the utmost sophistication; in the midst of its wildest extravagances there is always a profound knowledge of music on tap, and a profound love of it to boot. Here, perhaps, more than anywhere else, Huneker's delight in the things he deals with is obvious. It is not a seminary that he keeps, but a sort of club of tone enthusiasts, and membership in it is infinitely charming.

§ 6

This capacity for making the thing described seem important and delightful, this quality of infectious gusto, this father-talent of all the talents that a critic needs, sets off his literary criticism no less than his discourse on music and musicians. Such a book as "Iconoclasts" or "Egoists" is full of useful information, but it is even more full of agreeable adventure. The style is the book, as it is the man. It is arch, staccato, ironical, witty, galloping, playful, polyglot, allusive—sometimes, alas, so allusive as to reduce the Drama Leaguer and women's clubber to wonderment and ire. In writing of plays or of books, as in writing of cities, tone-poems or philosophies, Huneker always assumes that the elements are already well-grounded, that he is dealing with the initiated, that a pause to explain would be an affront. Sad work for the Philistines—but a joy to the elect! All this polyphonic allusiveness, this intricate fuguing of ideas, is not to be confused, remember, with the hollow showiness of the academic soothsayer. It is as natural to the man, as much a part of him as the clanging Latin of Johnson, or, to leap from art to art Huneker-wise, the damnable cross-rhythms of Brahms. He could no more write without his stock company of heretic sages than he could write without his ration of malt. And, on examination, all of them turned out to be real. They are far up dark alleys, but they are there! . . . And one finds them, at last, to be as pleasant company as the multilingual puns of Nietzsche or Debussy's chords of the second.

As for the origin of that style, it seems to have a complex ancestry. Huneker's first love was Poe, and even today he still casts affectionate glances in that direction, but there is surely nothing of Poe's elephantine labouring in his skipping, *pizzicato* sentences. Then came Carlyle—the Carlyle of "Sartor Resartus"—a god long forgotten. Huneker's mother was a woman of taste; on reading his first scribblings, she gave him Cardinal Newman, and bade him consider the Queen's English. Newman achieved a useful purging; the style that remained was ready for Flaubert. From the author of "L'Education Sentimentale," I daresay, came the deciding influence, with Nietzsche's staggering brilliance offering suggestions later on. Thus Huneker, as stylist, owes nearly all to France, for Nietzsche, too, learned how to write there, and to the end of his days he always wrote more like a Frenchman than a German. His greatest service to his own country, indeed, was not as anarch, but as teacher of writing. He taught the Germans that their language had a snap in it as well as sighs and gargles—that it was possible to write German and yet not wander in a wood. There are whole pages of Nietzsche that suggest such things, say, as the essay on Maurice Barrès in "Egoists," with its bold tropes, its rapid gait, its sharp *sforzandos.* And you will find old Friedrich at his tricks from end to end of "Old Fogy."

Of the actual contents of such books as "Egoists" and "Iconoclasts" it is unnecessary to say anything. One no longer reads them for their matter, but for their manner. Every flapper now knows all that is worth knowing about Ibsen, Strindberg, Maeterlinck and Shaw, and a great deal that is not worth knowing. We have disentangled Hauptmann from Sudermann, and, thanks to Dr. Lewisohn, may read all his plays in English. Even Henry Becque has got into the vulgate and is familiar to the Drama League. As for Anatole France, his "Revolt of the Angels" is on the shelves of the Carnegie Libraries, and the Comstocks have let it pass. New gods whoop and rage in Valhalla: Verhaeren, Artzibashef, Przybyszewski. Huneker, alas, seems to drop behind the procession. He writes nothing about these second-hand third-raters. He has come to Wedekind, Schnitzler, Schoenberg, Korngold and Moussorgsky, and he has discharged a few rounds of shrapnel at the Gallo-Asiatic petticoat philosopher, Henri Bergson, but here he has stopped, as he has stopped at Matisse, Picasso, Epstein and Augustus John in painting. As he says himself, "one must get off somewhere." . . .

Particularly if one grows weary of criticism—and in Huneker, of late, I detect more than one sign of weariness. Youth is behind him, and with it some of its zest for exploration and combat. "The pathos of distance" is a phrase that haunts him as poignantly as it haunted Nietzsche, its maker. Not so long ago I tried to induce him to write some new Old Fogy sketches, nominating Puccini, Strawinsky, Schoenberg, Korngold, Elgar. He protested that the mood was gone from him forever, that he could not turn the clock back twenty years. His late work in *Puck*, the *Times* and the *Sun*, shows an unaccustomed acquiescence in current valuations. He praises such one-day masterpieces as McFee's "Casuals of the Sea"; he is polite to the gaudy heroines of the opera-house; he gags a bit at Wright's "Modern Painting"; he actually makes a gingery curtsy to Frank Jewett Mather, a Princeton professor. . . . The pressure in the gauges can't keep up to 250 pounds forever. Man must tire of fighting after awhile, and seek his ease in his inn. . . .

Perhaps the post-bellum transvaluation of all values will bring Huneker to his feet again, and with something of the old glow and gusto in him. And if the new men do not stir up, then assuredly the wrecks of the ancient cities will: the Paris of his youth; Munich, Dresden, Vienna, Brussels, London; above all, Prague. Go to "New Cosmopolis" and you will find where his heart lies, or, if not his heart, then at all events his oesophagus and pylorus. . . . Here, indeed, the thread of his meditations is a thread of nutriment. However diverted by the fragrance of the Dutch woods, the church bells of Belgium, the music of Stuttgart, the bad pictures of Dublin, the plays of Paris, the musty romance of old Wien, he always comes back anon to such ease as a man may find in his inn. "The stomach of Vienna," he says, "first interested me, not its soul." And so, after a dutiful genuflexion to St. Stephen's ("Old Steffel," as the Viennese call it), he proceeds to investigate the paprika-chicken, the *Gulyas*, the *Risi-bisi*, the *Apfelstrudel*, the *Kaiserschmarrn* and the native and authentic *Wienerschnitzel*. And from food to drink—specifically, to the haunts of Pilsner, to "certain semi-sacred houses where the ritual of beer-drinking is observed," to the shrines at which beer maniacs meet, to "a little old house near a Greek church" where "the best-kept Pilsner in Vienna may be found."

The best-kept Pilsner in Vienna! The phrase enchants like an entrance of the horns. The best caviare in Russia, the worst actor on Broadway, the most virtuous angel in Heaven! Such superlatives are transcendental. And yet,—so rare is perfection in this world!—the news swiftly follows, unexpected, disconcerting, that the best Pilsner in Vienna is far short of the ideal. For some undetermined reason—the influence of the American tourist? the decay of the Austrian national character?—the Vienna *Bierwirte* freeze and paralyze it with too much ice, so that it chills the nerves it should caress, and fills the heart below with heaviness and repining. Avoid Vienna, says Huneker, if you are one who understands and venerates the great Bohemian brew! And if, deluded, you find yourself there, take the first *D-zug* for Prague, that lovely city, for in it you will find the Pilsen *Urquell,* and in the Pilsen *Urquell* you will find the best Pilsner in Christendom—its colour a phosphorescent, translucent, golden yellow, its foam like whipped cream, its temperature exactly and invariably right. Not even at Pilsen itself (which the Bohemians call Plezen) is the emperor of malt liquors more stupendously grateful to the palate. Write it down before you forget: the Pilsen *Urquell,* Prague, Bohemia, 120 miles S. S. E. of Dresden, on the river Moldau (which the natives call the Vitava). Ask for Fräulein Ottilie. Mention the name of Herr Huneker, the American *Schriftsteller.*

Of all the eminent and noble cities between the Alleghenies and the Balkans, Prague seems to be Huneker's favourite. He calls it poetic, precious, delectable, original, dramatic—a long string of adjectives, each argued for with eloquence that is unmistakably sincere. He stands fascinated before the towers and pinnacles of the Hradschin, "a miracle of tender rose and marble white with golden spots of sunshine that would have made Claude Monet envious." He pays his devotions to the Chapel of St. Wenceslaus, "crammed with the bones of buried kings," or, at any rate, to the shrine of St. John Nepomucane, "composed of nearly two tons of silver." He is charmed by the beauty of the stout, black-haired, red-cheeked Bohemian girls, and hopes that enough of them will emigrate to the United States to improve the fading pulchritude of our own houris. But most of all, he has praises for the Bohemian cuisine, with its incomparable apple tarts, and its dumplings of cream cheese, and for the magnificent, the overpowering, the ineffable Pilsner of Prague. This Pilsner motive runs through the book from cover to cover. In the midst of Dutch tulip-beds, Dublin cobblestones, Madrid sunlight and Atlantic City leg-shows, one hears it insistently, deep down in the orchestra. The cellos weave it into the polyphony, sometimes clearly, sometimes in scarcely recognizable augmentation. It is heard again in the wood-wind; the bassoons grunt it thirstily; it slides around in the violas; it rises to a stately choral in the brass.

And chiefly it is in minor. Chiefly it is sounded by one who longs for the Pilsen *Urquell* in a far land, and among a barbarous and teetotaling people, and in an atmosphere as hostile to the recreations of the palate as it is to the recreations of the intellect.

As I say, this Huneker is a foreigner and hence accursed. There is something about him as exotic as a samovar, as essentially un-American as a bashi-bazouk, a nose-ring or a fugue. He is filled to the throttle with strange and unnational heresies. He ranks Beethoven miles above the native gods, and not only Beethoven, but also Bach and Brahms, and not only Bach and Brahms, but also Berlioz, Bizet, Bruch and Bülow and perhaps even Balakirew, Bellini, Balfe, Borodin and Boïeldieu. He regards Budapest as a more civilized city than his native Philadelphia, Stendhal as a greater literary artist than Washington Irving, "Künstler Leben" as better music than "There is Sunlight in My Soul." Irish? I still doubt it, despite the *Stammbaum.* Who ever heard of an Irish epicure, an Irish *flâneur*, or, for that matter, an Irish contrapuntist? The arts of the voluptuous category are unknown west of Cherbourg; one leaves them behind with the French pilot. Even the Czech-Irish hypothesis (or is it Magyar-Irish?) has a smell of the lamp. Perhaps it should be Irish-Czech. . . .

§ 7

There remain the books of stories, "Visionaries" and "Melomaniacs." It is not surprising to hear that both are better liked in France and Germany than in England and the United States. ("Visionaries" has even appeared in Bohemian.) Both are made up of what the Germans call *Kultur-Novellen*—that is, stories dealing, not with the emotions common to all men, but with the clash of ideas among the civilized and godless minority. In some of them, *e.g.*, "Rebels of the Moon," what one finds is really not a story at all, but a static discussion, half aesthetic and half lunatic. In others, *e.g.*, "Isolde's Mother," the whole action revolves around an assumption incomprehensible to the general. One can scarcely imagine most of these tales in the magazines. They would puzzle and outrage the readers of Gouverneur Morris and Gertrude Atherton, and the readers of Howells and Mrs. Wharton no less. Their point of view is essentially the aesthetic one; the overwhelming importance of beauty is never in any doubt. And the beauty thus vivisected and fashioned into new designs is never the simple Wordsworthian article, of fleecy clouds and primroses all compact; on the contrary, it is the highly artificial beauty of pigments and tone-colours, of Cézanne landscapes and the second act of "Tristan und Isolde," of Dunsanyan dragons and Paracelsian mysteries. Here, indeed, Huneker riots in the aesthetic occultism that he loves. Music slides over into diabolism; the Pobloff symphony rends the firmament of Heaven; the ghost of Chopin drives Mychowski to drink; a single drum-beat finishes the estimable consort of the composer of the Tympani symphony. In "The Eighth Deadly Sin" we have a paean to perfume—the only one, so far as I know, in English. In "The Hall of the Missing Footsteps" we behold the reaction of hasheesh upon Chopin's ballade in F major. . . . Strangely-flavoured, unearthly, perhaps unhealthy stuff. I doubt that it will ever be studied for its style in our new Schools of Literature; a devilish cunning if often there, but it leaves a smack of the pharmacopoeia. However, as George Gissing used to say, "the artist should be free from everything like moral prepossession." This lets in the Antichrist. . . .

Huneker himself seems to esteem these fantastic tales above all his other work. Story-writing, indeed, was his first love, and his Opus 1, a bad imitation of Poe, by name "The Comet," was done in

Philadelphia so long ago as July 4, 1876. (Temperature, 105 degrees Fahrenheit.) One rather marvels that he has never attempted a novel. It would have been as bad, perhaps, as "Love Among the Artists," but certainly no bore. He might have given George Moore useful help with "Evelyn Innes" and "Sister Teresa": they are about music, but not by a musician. As for me, I see no great talent for fiction *qua* fiction in these two volumes of exotic tales. They are interesting simply because Huneker the story teller so often yields place to Huneker the playboy of the arts. Such things as "Antichrist" and "The Woman Who Loved Chopin" are no more, at bottom, than second-rate anecdotes; it is the filling, the sauce, the embroidery that counts. But what filling! What sauce! What embroidery! . . . One never sees more of Huneker. . . .

§ 8

He must stand or fall, however, as critic. It is what he has written about other men, not what he has concocted himself, that makes a figure of him, and gives him his unique place in the sterile literature of the republic's second century. He stands for a *Weltanschauung* that is not only un-national, but anti-national; he is the chief of all the curbers and correctors of the American Philistine; in praising the arts he has also criticized a civilization. In the large sense, of course, he has had but small influence. After twenty years of earnest labour, he finds himself almost as alone as a Methodist in Bavaria. The body of native criticism remains as I have described it; an endless piling up of platitudes, an homeric mass of false assumptions and jejune conclusions, an insane madness to reduce beauty to terms of a petty and pornographic morality. One might throw a thousand bricks in any American city without striking a single man who could give an intelligible account of either Hauptmann or Cézanne, or of the reasons for holding Schumann to have been a better composer than Mendelssohn. The boys in our colleges are still taught that Whittier was a great poet and Fennimore Cooper a great novelist. Nine-tenths of our people—perhaps ninety-nine hundredths of our native-born—have yet to see their first good picture, or to hear their first symphony. Our Chamberses and Richard Harding Davises are national figures; our Norrises and Dreisers are scarcely tolerated. Of the two undoubted world figures that we have contributed to letters, one was allowed to die like a stray cat up an alley and the other was mistaken for a cheap buffoon. Criticism, as the average American "intellectual" understands it, is what a Frenchman, a German or a Russian would call donkeyism. In all the arts we still cling to the ideals of the dissenting pulpit, the public cemetery, the electric sign, the bordello parlour.

But for all that, I hang to a somewhat battered optimism, and one of the chief causes of that optimism is the fact that Huneker, after all these years, yet remains unhanged. A picturesque and rakish fellow, a believer in joy and beauty, a disdainer of petty bombast and moralizing, a sworn friend of all honest purpose and earnest striving, he has given his life to a work that must needs bear fruit hereafter. While the college pedagogues of the Brander Matthews type still worshipped the dead bones of Scribe and Sardou, Robertson and Bulwer-Lytton, he preached the new and revolutionary gospel of Ibsen. In the golden age of Rosa Bonheur's "The Horse Fair," he was expounding the principles of the post-impressionists. In the midst of the Sousa marches he whooped for Richard Strauss. Before the rev. professors had come to Schopenhauer, or even to Spencer, he was hauling ashore the devil-fish, Nietzsche. No stranger poisons have ever passed through the customs than those he has brought in his baggage. No man among us has ever urged more ardently, or with sounder knowledge or greater persuasiveness, that catholicity of taste and sympathy which stands in such direct opposition to the booming certainty and snarling narrowness of Little Bethel.

If he bears a simple label, indeed, it is that of anti-Philistine. And the Philistine he attacks is not so much the vacant and harmless fellow who belongs to the Odd Fellows and recreates himself with *Life* and *Leslie's Weekly* in the barber shop, as that more belligerent and pretentious donkey who presumes to do battle for "honest" thought and a "sound" ethic—the "forward looking" man, the university ignoramus, the conservator of orthodoxy, the rattler of ancient phrases—what Nietzsche called "the Philistine of culture." It is against this fat milch cow of wisdom that Huneker has brandished a spear since first there was a Huneker. He is a sworn foe to "the traps that snare the attention from poor or mediocre workmanship—the traps of sentimentalism, of false feeling, of cheap pathos, of the cheap moral." He is on the trail of those pious mountebanks who "clutter the market-places with their booths, mischievous half-art and tubs of tripe and soft soap." Superficially, as I say, he seems to have made little progress in this benign *pogrom.* But under the surface, concealed from a first glance, he has undoubtedly left a mark

—faint, perhaps, but still a mark. To be a civilized man in America is measurably less difficult, despite the war, than it used to be, say, in 1890. One may at least speak of "Die Walküre" without being laughed at as a half-wit, and read Stirner without being confused with Castro and Raisuli, and argue that Huxley got the better of Gladstone without being challenged at the polls. I know of no man who pushed in that direction harder than James Huneker.

IV. PURITANISM AS A LITERARY FORCE

IV

PURITANISM AS A LITERARY FORCE

§ 1

CALVINISM," says Dr. Leon Kellner, in his excellent little history of American literature,[1] "is the natural theology of the disinherited; it never flourished, therefore, anywhere as it did in the barren hills of Scotland and in the wilds of North America." The learned doctor is here speaking of theology in what may be called its narrow technical sense—that is, as a theory of God. Under Calvinism, in the New World as well as in the Old, it became no more than a luxuriant demonology; even God himself was transformed into a superior sort of devil, ever wary and wholly merciless. That primitive demonology still survives in the barbaric doctrines of the Methodists and Baptists, particularly in the South; but it has been ameliorated, even there, by a growing sense of the divine grace, and so the old God of Plymouth Rock, as practically conceived,

[1] American Literature, tr. by Julia Franklin; New York, Doubleday, Page and Co., 1915.

is now scarcely worse than the average jail warden or Italian padrone. On the ethical side, however, Calvinism is dying a much harder death, and we are still a long way from the enlightenment. Save where Continental influences have measurably corrupted the Puritan idea—*e.g.*, in such cities as New York, San Francisco and New Orleans,—the prevailing American view of the world and its mysteries is still a moral one, and no other human concern gets half the attention that is endlessly lavished upon the problem of conduct, particularly of the other fellow. It needed no official announcement to define the function and office of the republic as that of an international expert in morals, and the mentor and exemplar of the more backward nations. Within, as well as without, the eternal rapping of knuckles and proclaiming of new austerities goes on. The American, save in moments of conscious and swiftly lamented deviltry, casts up all ponderable values, including even the values of beauty, in terms of right and wrong. He is beyond all things else, a judge and a policeman; he believes firmly that there is a mysterious power in law; he supports and embellishes its operation with a fanatical vigilance.

Naturally enough, this moral obsession has given a strong colour to American literature. In truth, it has coloured it so brilliantly that American literature is set off sharply from all other literatures. In none other will you find so wholesale and ecstatic a sacrifice of aesthetic ideas, of all the fine gusto of passion and beauty, to notions of what is meet, proper and nice. From the books of grisly sermons that were the first American contribution to letters down to that amazing literature of "inspiration" which now flowers so prodigiously, with two literary ex-Presidents among its chief virtuosi, one observes no relaxation of the moral pressure. In the history of every other literature there have been periods of what might be called moral innocence—periods in which a naif *joie de vivre* has broken through all concepts of duty and responsibility, and the wonder and glory of the universe have been hymned with unashamed zest. The age of Shakespeare comes to mind at once: the violence of the Puritan reaction offers a measure of the pendulum's wild swing. But in America no such general rising of the blood has ever been seen. The literature of the nation, even the literature of the enlightened minority, has been under harsh Puritan restraints from the beginning, and despite a few stealthy efforts at revolt—usually quite without artistic value or even common honesty, as in the case of the cheap fiction magazines and that of smutty plays on Broadway, and always very short-lived—it shows not the slightest sign of emancipating itself today. The American, try as he will, can never imagine any work of the imagination as wholly devoid of moral content. It must either tend toward the promotion of virtue, or be suspect and abominable.

If any doubt of this is in your mind, turn to the critical articles in the newspapers and literary weeklies; you will encounter enough proofs in a month's explorations to convince you forever. A novel or a play is judged among us, not by its dignity of conception, its artistic honesty, its perfection of workmanship, but almost entirely by its orthodoxy of doctrine, its platitudinousness, its usefulness as a moral tract. A digest of the reviews of such a book as David Graham Phillips' "Susan Lenox" or of such a play as Ibsen's "Hedda Gabler" would make astounding reading for a Continental European. Not only the childish incompetents who write for the daily press, but also most of our critics of experience and reputation, seem quite unable to estimate a piece of writing as a piece of writing, a work of art as a work of art; they almost inevitably drag in irrelevant gabble as to whether this or that personage in it is respectable, or this or that situation in accordance with the national notions of what is edifying and nice. Fully nine-tenths of the reviews of Dreiser's "The Titan," without question the best American novel of its year, were devoted chiefly to indignant denunciations of the morals of Frank Cowperwood, its central character. That the man was superbly imagined and magnificently depicted, that he stood out from the book in all the flashing vigour of life, that his creation was an artistic achievement of a very high and difficult order—these facts seem to have made no impression upon the reviewers whatever. They were Puritans writing for Puritans, and all they could see in Cowperwood was an anti-Puritan, and in his creator another. It will remain for Europeans, I daresay, to discover the true stature of "The Titan," as it remained for Europeans to discover the true stature of "Sister Carrie."

Just how deeply this corrective knife has cut you may find plainly displayed in Dr. Kellner's little book. He sees the throttling influence of an ever alert and bellicose Puritanism, not only in our grand literature, but also in our petit literature, our minor poetry, even in our humour. The Puritan's utter lack of aesthetic sense, his distrust of all romantic emotion, his unmatchable intolerance of opposition, his unbreakable belief in his own bleak and narrow views, his savage cruelty of attack, his lust for relentless and barbarous persecution—these things have put an almost unbearable burden upon the exchange of ideas in the United States, and particularly upon that form of it which involves playing with them for the mere game's sake. On the one hand, the writer who would deal seriously and honestly with the larger problems of life, particularly in the rigidly-partitioned ethical field, is restrained by laws that would have kept a Balzac or a Zola in prison from year's end to year's end; and on the other hand the writer who would proceed against the reigning superstitions by mockery has been silenced by taboos that are quite as stringent, and by an indifference that is even worse. For all our professed delight in and capacity for jocosity, we have produced so far but one genuine wit—Ambrose Bierce—and, save to a small circle, he remains unknown today. Our great humourists, including even Mark Twain, have had to take protective colouration, whether willingly or unwillingly, from the prevailing ethical foliage, and so one finds them levelling their darts, not at the stupidities of the Puritan majority, but at the evidences of lessening stupidity in the anti-Puritan minority. In other words, they have done battle, not against, but *for* Philistinism—and

Philistinism is no more than another name for Puritanism. Both wage a ceaseless warfare upon beauty in its every form, from painting to religious ritual, and from the drama to the dance—the first because it holds beauty to be a mean and stupid thing, and the second because it holds beauty to be distracting and corrupting.

Mark Twain, without question, was a great artist; there was in him something of that prodigality of imagination, that aloof engrossment in the human comedy, that penetrating cynicism, which one associates with the great artists of the Renaissance. But his nationality hung around his neck like a millstone; he could never throw off his native Philistinism. One ploughs through "The Innocents Abroad" and through parts of "A Tramp Abroad" with incredulous amazement. Is such coarse and ignorant clowning to be accepted as humour, as great humour, as the best humour that the most humorous of peoples has produced? Is it really the mark of a smart fellow to lift a peasant's cackle over "Lohengrin"? Is Titian's chromo of Moses in the bullrushes seriously to be regarded as the noblest picture in Europe? Is there nothing in Latin Christianity, after all, save petty grafting, monastic scandals and the worship of the knuckles and shin-bones of dubious saints?

May not a civilized man, disbelieving in it, still find himself profoundly moved by its dazzling history, the lingering remnants of its old magnificence, the charm of its gorgeous and melancholy loveliness? In the presence of all beauty of man's creation—in brief, of what we roughly call art, whatever its form—the voice of Mark Twain was the voice of the Philistine. A literary artist of very high rank himself, with instinctive gifts that lifted him, in "Huckleberry Finn" to kinship with Cervantes and Aristophanes, he was yet so far the victim of his nationality that he seems to have had no capacity for distinguishing between the good and the bad in the work of other men of his own craft. The literary criticism that one occasionally finds in his writings is chiefly trivial and ignorant; his private inclination appears to have been toward such romantic sentimentality as entrances school-boys; the thing that interested him in Shakespeare was not the man's colossal genius, but the absurd theory that Bacon wrote his plays. Had he been born in France (the country of his chief abomination!) instead of in a Puritan village of the American hinterland, I venture that he would have conquered the world. But try as he would, being what he was, he could not get rid of the Puritan smugness and cocksureness, the Puritan distrust of new ideas, the

Puritan incapacity for seeing beauty as a thing in itself, and the full peer of the true and the good.

It is, indeed, precisely in the works of such men as Mark Twain that one finds the best proofs of the Puritan influence in American letters, for it is there that it is least expected and hence most significant. Our native critics, unanimously Puritans themselves, are anaesthetic to the flavour, but to Dr. Kellner, with his half-European, half-Oriental culture, it is always distinctly perceptible. He senses it, not only in the harsh Calvinistic fables of Hawthorne and the pious gurglings of Longfellow, but also in the poetry of Bryant, the tea-party niceness of Howells, the "maiden-like reserve" of James Lane Allen, and even in the work of Joel Chandler Harris. What! A Southern Puritan? Well, why not? What could be more erroneous than the common assumption that Puritanism is exclusively a Northern, a New England, madness? The truth is that it is as thoroughly national as the kindred belief in the devil, and runs almost unobstructed from Portland to Portland and from the Lakes to the Gulf. It is in the South, indeed, and not in the North, that it takes on its most bellicose and extravagant forms. Between the upper tier of New England and the Potomac river there was not a single prohibition state—but thereafter, alas, they came in huge blocks! And behind that infinitely prosperous Puritanism there is a long and unbroken tradition. Berkeley, the last of the Cavaliers, was kicked out of power in Virginia so long ago as 1650. Lord Baltimore, the Proprietor of Maryland, was brought to terms by the Puritans of the Severn in 1657. The Scotch Covenanter, the most uncompromising and unenlightened of all Puritans, flourished in the Carolinas from the start, and in 1698, or thereabout, he was reinforced from New England. In 1757 a band of Puritans invaded what is now Georgia—and Georgia has been a Puritan barbarism ever since. Even while the early (and half-mythical) Cavaliers were still in nominal control of all these Southern plantations, they clung to the sea-coast. The population that moved down the chain of the Appalachians during the latter part of the eighteenth century, and then swept over them into the Mississippi valley, was composed almost entirely of Puritans—chiefly intransigeants from New England (where Unitarianism was getting on its legs), kirk-crazy Scotch, and that plupious and beauty-hating folk, the Scotch-Irish. "In the South today," said John Fiske a generation ago, "there is more Puritanism surviving than in New England." In that whole region, an area three times as large as France or

Germany, there is not a single orchestra capable of playing Beethoven's C minor symphony, or a single painting worth looking at, or a single public building or monument of any genuine distinction, or a single factory devoted to the making of beautiful things, or a single poet, novelist, historian, musician, painter or sculptor whose reputation extends beyond his own country. Between the Mason and Dixon line and the mouth of the Mississippi there is but one opera-house, and that one was built by a Frenchman, and is now, I believe, closed. The only domestic art this huge and opulent empire knows is in the hands of Mexican greasers; its only native music it owes to the despised negro; its only genuine poet was permitted to die up an alley like a stray dog.

§ 2

In studying the anatomy and physiology of American Puritanism, and its effects upon the national literature, one quickly discerns two main streams of influence. On the one hand, there is the influence of the original Puritans—whether of New England or of the South—, who came to the New World with a ready-made philosophy of the utmost clarity, positiveness and inclusiveness of scope, and who attained to such a position of political and intellectual leadership that they were able to force it almost unchanged upon the whole population, and to endow it with such vitality that it successfully resisted alien opposition later on. And on the other hand, one sees a complex of social and economic conditions which worked in countless irresistible ways against the rise of that dionysian spirit, that joyful acquiescence in life, that philosophy of the *Ja-sager,* which offers to Puritanism, today as in times past, its chief and perhaps only effective antagonism. In other words, the American of the days since the Revolution has had Puritanism diligently pressed upon him from without, and at the same time he has led, in the main, a life that has engendered a chronic hospitality to it, or at all events to its salient principles, within.

Dr. Kellner accurately describes the process whereby the aesthetic spirit, and its concomitant spirit of joy, were squeezed out of the original New Englanders, so that no trace of it showed in their literature, or even in their lives, for a century and a half after the first settlements. "Absorption in God," he says, "seems incompatible with the presentation (*i.e.*, aesthetically) of mankind. The God of the Puritans was in this respect a jealous God who brooked no sort of creative rivalry. The inspired moments of the loftiest souls were filled with the thought of God and His designs; spiritual life was wholly dominated by solicitude regarding salvation, the hereafter, grace; how could such petty concerns as personal experience of a lyric nature, the transports or the pangs of love, find utterance? What did a lyric occurrence like the first call of the cuckoo, elsewhere so welcome, or the first sight of the snowdrop, signify compared with the last Sunday's sermon and the new interpretation of the old riddle of evil in the world? And apart from the fact that everything of a personal nature must have appeared so trivial, all the sources of secular lyric poetry were offensive and impious to Puritan theology. . . . One thing is an established fact: up to the close of the eighteenth century America had no belletristic literature."

This Puritan bedevilment by the idea of personal sin, this reign of the God-crazy, gave way in later years, as we shall see, to other and somewhat milder forms of pious enthusiam. At the time of the Revolution, indeed, the importation of French political ideas was accompanied by an importation of French theological ideas, and such men as Franklin and Jefferson dallied with what, in those days at least, was regarded as downright atheism. Even in New England this influence made itself felt; there was a gradual letting down of Calvinism to the softness of Unitarianism, and that change was presently to flower in the vague temporizing of Transcendentalism. But as Puritanism, in the strict sense, declined in virulence and took deceptive new forms, there was a compensating growth of its brother, Philistinism, and by the first quarter of the nineteenth century, the distrust of beauty, and of the joy that is its object, was as firmly established throughout the land as it had ever been in New England. The original Puritans had at least been men of a certain education, and even of a certain austere culture. They were inordinately hostile to beauty in all its forms, but one somehow suspects that much of their hostility was due to a sense of their weakness before it, a realization of its disarming psychical pull. But the American of the new republic was of a different kidney. He was not so much hostile to beauty as devoid of any consciousness of it; he stood as unmoved before its phenomena as a savage before a table of logarithms. What he had set up on this continent, in brief, was a commonwealth of peasants and small traders, a paradise of the third-rate, and its national philosophy, almost wholly unchecked by the more sophisticated and civilized ideas of an aristocracy, was precisely the philosophy that one finds among peasants and small traders at all times and everywhere. The difference between the United States and any other nation did not lie in any essential difference between American peasants and other peasants, but simply in the fact that here, alone, the voice of the peasant was the single voice of the nation—that here, alone, the only way to eminence and public influence was the way of acquiescence in the opinions and prejudices of the untutored and Philistine mob. Jackson was the *Stammvater* of the new statesmen and philosophers; he carried the mob's distrust of good taste even into the field of conduct; he was the first to put the rewards of conformity above the dictates of common decency; he founded a whole hierarchy of Philistine messiahs, the roaring of which still belabours the ear.

Once established, this culture of the intellectually disinherited tended to defend and perpetuate itself. On the one hand, there was no appearance of a challenge from within, for the exigent problems of existence in a country that was yet but half settled and organized left its people with no energy for questioning what at least satisfied their gross needs, and so met the pragmatic test. And on the other hand, there was no critical pressure from without, for the English culture which alone reached over the sea was itself entering upon its Victorian decline, and the influence of the native aristocracy—the degenerating *Junkers* of the great estates and the boorish magnates of the city *bourgeoisie*—was quite without any cultural direction at all. The chief concern of the American people, even above the bread-and-butter question, was politics. They were incessantly hag-ridden by political difficulties, both internal and external, of an inordinate complexity, and these occupied all the leisure they could steal from the sordid work of everyday. More, their new and troubled political ideas tended to absorb all the rancorous certainty of their fading religious ideas, so that devotion to a theory or a candidate became translated into devotion to a revelation, and the game of politics turned itself into a holy war. The custom of connecting purely political doctrines with pietistic concepts of an inflammable nature, then firmly set up by skilful persuaders of the mob, has never quite died out in the United States. There has not been a presidential contest since Jackson's day without its Armageddons, its marching of Christian soldiers, its crosses of gold, its crowns of thorns. The most successful American politicians, beginning with the anti-slavery agitators, have been those most adept at twisting the ancient gauds and shibboleths of Puritanism to partisan uses. Every campaign that we have seen for eighty years has been, on each side, a pursuit of bugaboos, a denunciation of heresies, a snouting up of immoralities.

But it was during the long contest against slavery, beginning with the appearance of William Lloyd Garrison's *Liberator* in 1831 and ending at Appomattox, that this gigantic supernaturalization of politics reached its most astounding heights. In those days, indeed, politics and religion coalesced in a manner not seen in the world since the Middle Ages, and the combined pull of the two was so powerful that none could quite resist it. All men of any ability and ambition turned to political activity for self-expression. It engaged the press to the exclusion of everything else; it conquered the pulpit; it even laid its hand upon industry and trade. Drawing the best imaginative talent into its service—Jefferson and Lincoln may well stand as examples—it left the cultivation of belles lettres, and of all the other arts no less, to women and admittedly second-rate men. And when, breaking through this taboo, some chance first-rate man gave himself over to purely aesthetic expression, his reward was not only neglect, but even a sort of ignominy, as if such enterprises were not fitting for males with hair on their chests. I need not point to Poe and Whitman, both disdained as dreamers and wasters, and both proceeded against with the utmost rigours of outraged Philistinism.

In brief, the literature of that whole period, as Algernon Tassin shows in "The Magazine in America," [1] was almost completely disassociated from life as men were then living it. Save one counts in such crude politico-puritan tracts as "Uncle Tom's Cabin," it is difficult to find a single contemporaneous work that interprets the culture of the time, or even accurately represents it. Later on, it found historians and anatomists, and in one work, at least, to wit, "Huckleberry Finn," it was studied and projected with the highest art, but no such impulse to make imaginative use of it showed itself contemporaneously, and there was not even the crude sentimentalization of here and now that one finds in the popular novels of today. Fenimore Cooper filled his romances, not with the people about him, but with the Indians beyond the sky-line, and made them half-fabulous to boot. Irving told fairy tales about the forgotten Knickerbockers; Hawthorne turned backward to the Puritans of Plymouth Rock; Longfellow to the Acadians and the prehistoric Indians; Emerson took flight from earth altogether; even Poe sought refuge in a

[1] New York, Dodd, Mead & Co., 1916.

land of fantasy. It was only the frank second-raters—*e.g.*, Whittier and Lowell—who ventured to turn to the life around them, and the banality of the result is a sufficient indication of the crudeness of the current taste, and the mean position assigned to the art of letters. This was pre-eminently the era of the moral tale, the Sunday-school book. Literature was conceived, not as a thing in itself, but merely as a hand-maiden to politics or religion. The great celebrity of Emerson in New England was not the celebrity of a literary artist, but that of a theologian and metaphysician; he was esteemed in much the same way that Jonathan Edwards had been esteemed. Even down to our own time, indeed, his vague and empty philosophizing has been put above his undeniable capacity for graceful utterance, and it remained for Dr. Kellner to consider him purely as a literary artist, and to give him due praise for his skill.

The Civil War brought that era of sterility to an end. As I shall show later on, the shock of it completely reorganized the American scheme of things, and even made certain important changes in the national Puritanism, or, at all events, in its machinery. Whitman, whose career straddled, so to speak, the four years of the war, was the leader—and for a long while, the only trooper—of a double revolt. On the one hand he offered a courageous challenge to the intolerable prudishness and dirty-mindedness of Puritanism, and on the other hand he boldly sought the themes and even the modes of expression of his poetry in the arduous, contentious and highly melodramatic life that lay all about him. Whitman, however, was clearly before his time. His countrymen could see him only as immoralist; save for a pitiful few of them, they were dead to any understanding of his stature as artist, and even unaware that such a category of men existed. He was put down as an invader of the public decencies, a disturber of the public peace; even his eloquent war poems, surely the best of all his work, were insufficient to get him a hearing; the sentimental rubbish of "The Blue and the Gray" and the ecstatic supernaturalism of "The Battle Hymn of the Republic" were far more to the public taste. Where Whitman failed, indeed, all subsequent explorers of the same field have failed with him, and the great war has left no more mark upon American letters than if it had never been fought. Nothing remotely approaching the bulk and beam of Tolstoi's "War and Peace," or, to descend to a smaller scale, Zola's "The Attack on the Mill," has come out of it. Its appeal to the national imagination was undoubtedly of the most profound character; it coloured politics for fifty years, and is today a dominating influence in the thought of whole sections of the American people. But in all that stirring up there was no upheaval of artistic consciousness, for the plain reason that there was no artistic consciousness there to heave up, and all we have in the way of Civil War literature is a few conventional melodramas, a few half-forgotten short stories by Ambrose Bierce and Stephen Crane, and a half dozen idiotic popular songs in the manner of Randall's "Maryland, My Maryland."

In the seventies and eighties, with the appearance of such men as Henry James, William Dean Howells, Mark Twain and Bret Harte, a better day seemed to be dawning. Here, after a full century of infantile romanticizing, were four writers who at least deserved respectful consideration as literary artists, and what is more, three of them turned from the conventionalized themes of the past to the teeming and colourful life that lay under their noses. But this promise of better things was soon found to be no more than a promise. Mark Twain, after "The Gilded Age," slipped back into romanticism tempered by Philistinism, and was presently in the era before the Civil War, and finally in the Middle Ages, and even beyond. Harte, a brilliant technician, had displayed his whole stock when he had displayed his technique: his stories were not even superficially true to the life they presumed to depict; one searched them in vain for an interpretation of it; they were simply idle tales. As for Howells and James, both quickly showed that timorousness and reticence which are the distinguishing marks of the Puritan, even in his most intellectual incarnations. The American scene that they depicted with such meticulous care was chiefly peopled with marionettes. They shrunk, characteristically, from those larger, harsher clashes of will and purpose which one finds in all truly first-rate literature. In particular, they shrunk from any interpretation of life which grounded itself upon an acknowledgment of its inexorable and inexplicable tragedy. In the vast combat of instincts and aspirations about them they saw only a feeble jousting of comedians, unserious and insignificant. Of the great questions that have agitated the minds of men in Howells' time one gets no more than a faint and far-away echo in his novels. His investigations, one may say, are carried on *in vacuo;* his discoveries are not expressed in terms of passion, but in terms of giggles.

In the followers of Howells and James one finds little save an empty imitation of their emptiness, a somewhat puerile parodying of their highly artful but essentially personal technique. To wade through the books of such characteristic American fictioneers as Frances Hodgson Burnett, Mary E. Wilkins Freeman, F. Hopkinson Smith, Alice Brown, James Lane Allen, Winston Churchill, Ellen Glasgow, Gertrude Atherton and Sarah Orne Jewett is to undergo an experience that is almost terrible. The flow of words is completely purged of ideas; in place of them one finds no more than a romantic restatement of all the old platitudes and formulae. To call such an emission of graceful poppycock a literature, of course, is to mouth an absurdity, and yet, if the college professors who write treatises on letters are to be believed, it is the best we have to show. Turn, for example, to "A History of American Literature Since 1870," by Prof. Fred Lewis Pattee, one of the latest and undoubtedly one of the least unintelligent of these books. In it the gifted pedagogue gives extended notice to no less than six of the nine writers I have mentioned, and upon all of them his verdicts are flattering. He bestows high praises, direct and indirect, upon Mrs. Freeman's "grim and austere" manner, her "repression," her entire lack of poetical illumination. He compares Miss Jewett to both Howells and Hawthorne, not to mention Mrs. Gaskell—and

Addison! He grows enthusiastic over a hollow piece of fine writing by Miss Brown. And he forgets altogether to mention Dreiser, or Sinclair, or Medill Patterson, or Harry Leon Wilson, or George Ade! . . .

So much for the best. The worst is beyond description. France has her Brieux and her Henry Bordeaux; Germany has her Mühlbach, her stars of the *Gartenlaube;* England contributes Caine, Corelli, Oppenheim and company. But it is in our country alone that banality in letters takes on the proportions of a national movement; it is only here that a work of the imagination is habitually judged by its sheer emptiness of ideas, its fundamental platitudinousness, its correspondence with the imbecility of mob thinking; it is only here that "glad" books run up sales of hundreds of thousands. Richard Harding Davis, with his ideals of a floorwalker; Gene Stratton-Porter, with her snuffling sentimentality; Robert W. Chambers, with his "society" romances for shop-girls; Irvin Cobb, with his laboured, *Ayers' Almanac* jocosity; the authors of the *Saturday Evening Post* school, with their heroic drummers and stockbrokers, their ecstatic celebration of the stupid, the sordid, the ignoble—these, after all, are our typical *literati.* The Puritan fear of ideas is the master of them all. Some of them, in truth, most of them, have undeniable talent; in a more favourable environment not a few of them might be doing sound work. But they see how small the ring is, and they make their tricks small to fit it. Not many of them ever venture a leg outside. The lash of the ringmaster is swift, and it stings damnably. . . .

I say not many; I surely do not mean none at all. As a matter of fact, there have been intermittent rebellions against the prevailing pecksniffery and sentimentality ever since the days of Irving and Hawthorne. Poe led one of them—as critic more than as creative artist. His scathing attacks upon the Gerald Stanley Lees, the Hamilton Wright Mabies and the George E. Woodberrys of his time keep a liveliness and appositeness that the years have not staled; his criticism deserves to be better remembered. Poe sensed the Philistine pull of a Puritan civilization as none had before him, and combated it with his whole artillery of rhetoric. Another rebel, of course, was Whitman; how he came to grief is too well known to need recalling. What is less familiar is the fact that both the *Atlantic Monthly* and the *Century* (first called *Scribner's*) were set up by men in revolt against the reign of mush, as *Putnam's* and the *Dial* had been before them. The salutatory of the *Dial*, dated

1840, stated the case against the national mugginess clearly. The aim of the magazine, it said, was to oppose "that rigour of our conventions of religion and education which is turning us to stone" and to give expression to "new views and the dreams of youth." Alas, for these brave *révoltés! Putnam's* succumbed to the circumambient rigours and duly turned to stone, and is now no more. The *Atlantic*, once so heretical, has become as respectable as the New York *Evening Post*. As for the *Dial*, it was until lately the very pope of orthodoxy and jealously guarded the college professors who read it from the pollution of ideas. Only the *Century* has kept the faith unbrokenly. It is, indeed, the one first-class American magazine that has always welcomed newcomers, and that maintains an intelligent contact with the literature that is in being, and that consistently tries to make the best terms possible with the dominant Philistinism. It cannot go the whole way without running into danger; let it be said to the credit of its editors that they have more than once braved that danger.

The tale might be lengthened. Mark Twain, in his day, felt the stirrings of revolt, and not all his Philistinism was sufficient to hold him altogether in check. If you want to find out about the struggle that went on within him, read the biography by

Albert Bigelow Paine, or, better still, "The Mysterious Stranger" and "What is Man?" Alive, he had his position to consider; dead, he now speaks out. In the preface to "What is Man?" dated 1905, there is a curious confession of his incapacity for defying the taboos which surrounded him. The studies for the book, he says, were begun "twenty-five or twenty-seven years ago"—the period of "A Tramp Abroad" and "The Prince and the Pauper." It was actually written "seven years ago"—that is, just after "Following the Equator" and "Personal Recollections of Joan of Arc." And why did it lie so long in manuscript, and finally go out stealthily, under a private imprint? [1] Simply because, as Mark frankly confesses, he "dreaded (*and could not bear*) the disapproval of the people around" him. He knew how hard his fight for recognition had been; he knew what direful penalties outraged orthodoxy could inflict; he had in him the somewhat pathetic discretion of a respectable family man. But, dead, he is safely beyond reprisal, and so, after a prudent interval, the faithful Paine begins printing books in which, writing knowingly behind six feet of earth, he could set down his true ideas without fear. Some day, perhaps, we shall

[1] The first edition for public sale did not appear until June, 1917, and in it the preface was suppressed.

have his microbe story, and maybe even his picture of the court of Elizabeth.

A sneer in Prof. Pattee's history, before mentioned, recalls the fact that Hamlin Garland was also a rebel in his day and bawled for the Truth with a capital T. That was in 1893. Two years later the guardians of the national rectitude fell afoul of "Rose of Dutchers' Coolly" and Garland began to think it over; today he devotes himself to the safer enterprise of chasing spooks; his name is conspicuously absent from the Dreiser Protest. Nine years before his brief offending John Hay had set off a discreet bomb in "The Bread-Winners"—anonymously because "my standing would be seriously compromised" by an avowal. Six years later Frank Norris shook up the Phelpses and Mores of the time with "McTeague." Since then there have been assaults timorous and assaults head-long—by Bierce, by Dreiser, by Phillips, by Fuller—by Mary MacLanes and by Upton Sinclairs—by ploughboy poets from the Middle West and by jitney geniuses in Greenwich Village—assaults gradually tapering off to a mere sophomoric brashness and deviltry. And all of them like snow-ballings of Verdun. All of them petered out and ineffectual. The normal, the typical American book of today is as fully a remouthing of old husks as the normal book of Griswold's day. The whole atmosphere of our literature, in William James' phrase, is "mawkish and dishwatery." Books are still judged among us, not by their form and organization as works of art, their accuracy and vividness as representations of life, their validity and perspicacity as interpretations of it, but by their conformity to the national prejudices, their accordance with set standards of niceness and propriety. The thing irrevocably demanded is a "sane" book; the ideal is a "clean," an "inspiring," a "glad" book.

§ 3

All this may be called the Puritan impulse from within. It is, indeed, but a single manifestation of one of the deepest prejudices of a religious and half-cultured people—the prejudice against beauty as a form of debauchery and corruption—the distrust of all ideas that do not fit readily into certain accepted axioms—the belief in the eternal validity of moral concepts—in brief, the whole mental sluggishness of the lower orders of men. But in addition to this internal resistance, there has been laid upon American letters the heavy hand of a Puritan authority from without, and no examination of the history and present condition of our literature could be of any value which did not take it constantly into account, and work out the means of its influence and operation. That authority, as I shall show, transcends both in power and in alertness the natural reactions of the national mind, and is incomparably more potent in combating ideas. It is supported by a body of law that is unmatched in any other country of Christendom, and it is exercised with a fanatical harshness and vigilance that make escape from its operations well nigh impossible. Some of its effects, both direct and indirect, I shall describe later, but before doing so it may be well to trace its genesis and development.

At bottom, of course, it rests upon the inherent Puritanism of the people; it could not survive a year if they were opposed to the principle visible in it. That deep-seated and uncorrupted Puritanism, that conviction of the pervasiveness of sin, of the supreme importance of moral correctness, of the need of savage and inquisitorial laws, has been a dominating force in American life since the very beginning. There has never been any question before the nation, whether political or economic, religious or military, diplomatic or sociological, which did not resolve itself, soon or late, into a purely moral question. Nor has there ever been any surcease of the spiritual eagerness which lay at the bottom of the original Puritan's moral obsession: the American has been, from the very start, a man genuinely interested in the eternal mysteries, and fearful of missing their correct solution. The frank theocracy of the New England colonies had scarcely succumbed to the libertarianism of a godless Crown before there came the Great Awakening of 1734, with its orgies of homiletics and its restoration of talmudism to the first place among polite sciences. The Revolution, of course, brought a set-back: the colonists faced so urgent a need of unity in politics that they declared a sort of *Treuga Dei* in religion, and that truce, armed though it was, left its imprint upon the First Amendment to the Constitution. But immediately the young Republic emerged from the stresses of adolescence, a missionary army took to the field again, and before long the Asbury revival was paling that of Whitefield, Wesley and Jonathan Edwards, not only in its hortatory violence but also in the length of its lists of slain.

Thereafter, down to the outbreak of the Civil War, the country was rocked again and again by furious attacks upon the devil. On the one hand, this great campaign took a purely theological form, with a hundred new and fantastic creeds as its fruits; on the other hand, it crystallized into the hysterical temperance movement of the 30's and 40's, which penetrated to the very floor of Congress and put "dry" laws upon the statute-books of ten States; and on the third hand, as it were, it established a prudery in speech and thought from which we are yet but half delivered. Such ancient and innocent words as "bitch" and "bastard" disappeared from the American language; Bartlett tells us, indeed, in his "Dictionary of Americanisms," [1] that even "bull" was softened to "male cow." This was the Golden Age of euphemism, as it was of euphuism; the worst inventions of the English mid-Victorians were adopted and improved. The word "woman" became a term of opprobrium, verging close upon downright libel; legs became the inimitable "limbs"; the stomach began to run from the "bosom" to the pelvic arch; pantaloons faded into "unmentionables"; the newspapers spun their parts of speech into such gossamer webs as "a statutory offence," "a house of questionable repute" and "an interesting condition." And meanwhile the Good Templars and Sons of Temperance swarmed in the land like a plague of celestial locusts. There was not a hamlet without its uni-

[1] Second edition; Boston, Little, Brown & Co., 1859, xxvi.

formed phalanx, its affecting exhibit of reformed drunkards. The Kentucky Legislature succumbed to a travelling recruiting officer, and two-thirds of the members signed the pledge. The National House of Representatives took recess after recess to hear eminent excoriators of the Rum Demon, and more than a dozen of its members forsook their duties to carry the new gospel to the bucolic heathen —the vanguard, one may note in passing, of the innumerable Chautauquan caravan of later years.

Beneath all this bubbling on the surface, of course, ran the deep and swift undercurrent of anti-slavery feeling—a tide of passion which historians now attempt to account for on economic grounds, but which showed no trace of economic origin while it lasted. Its true quality was moral, devout, ecstatic; it culminated, to change the figure, in a supreme discharge of moral electricity, almost fatal to the nation. The crack of that great spark emptied the jar; the American people forgot all about their pledges and pruderies during the four years of Civil War. The Good Templars, indeed, were never heard of again, and with them into memory went many other singular virtuosi of virtue—for example, the Millerites. But almost before the last smoke of battle cleared away, a renaissance of Puritan ardour began, and by the middle of the 70's it was in full flower. Its high points and flashing lighthouses halt the backward-looking eye; the Moody and Sankey uproar, the triumphal entry of the Salvation Army, the recrudescence of the temperance agitation and its culmination in prohibition, the rise of the Young Men's Christian Association and of the Sunday-school, the almost miraculous growth of the Christian Endeavour movement, the beginnings of the vice crusade, the renewed injection of moral conceptions and rages into party politics (the "crime" of 1873!), the furious preaching of baroque Utopias, the invention of muckraking, the mad, glad war of extermination upon the Mormons, the hysteria over the Breckenridge-Pollard case and other like causes, the enormous multiplication of moral and religious associations, the spread of zoöphilia, the attack upon Mammon, the dawn of the uplift, and last but far from least, comstockery.

In comstockery, if I do not err, the new Puritanism gave a sign of its formal departure from the old, and moral endeavour suffered a general overhauling and tightening of the screws. The difference between the two forms is very well represented by the difference between the program of the half-forgotten Good Templars and the program set forth in the Webb Law of 1913, or by that between the somewhat diffident prudery of the 40's and the astoundingly ferocious and uncompromising vice-crusading of today. In brief, a difference between the *re*nunciation and *de*nunciation, asceticism and Mohammedanism, the hair shirt and the flaming sword. The distinguishing mark of the elder Puritanism, at least after it had attained to the stature of a national philosophy, was its appeal to the individual conscience, its exclusive concern with the elect, its strong flavour of self-accusing. Even the rage against slavery was, in large measure, an emotion of the mourners' bench. The thing that worried the more ecstatic Abolitionists was their sneaking sense of responsibility, the fear that they themselves were flouting the fire by letting slavery go on. The thirst to punish the concrete slave-owner, as an end in itself, did not appear until opposition had added exasperation to fervour. In most of the earlier harangues against his practice, indeed, you will find a perfect willingness to grant that slave-owner's good faith, and even to compensate him for his property. But the new Puritanism—or, perhaps more accurately, considering the shades of prefixes, the neo-Puritanism—is a frank harking back to the primitive spirit. The original Puritan of the bleak New England coast was not content to flay his own wayward carcass:

full satisfaction did not sit upon him until he had jailed a Quaker. That is to say, the sinner who excited his highest zeal and passion was not so much himself as his neighbour; to borrow a term from psychopathology, he was less the masochist than the sadist. And it is that very peculiarity which sets off his descendant of today from the ameliorated Puritan of the era between the Revolution and the Civil War. The new Puritanism is not ascetic, but militant. Its aim is not to lift up saints but to knock down sinners. Its supreme manifestation is the vice crusade, an armed pursuit of helpless outcasts by the whole military and naval forces of the Republic. Its supreme hero is Comstock Himself, with his pious boast that the sinners he jailed during his astounding career, if gathered into one penitential party, would have filled a train of sixty-one coaches, allowing sixty to the coach.

So much for the general trend and tenor of the movement. At the bottom of it, it is plain, there lies that insistent presentation of the idea of sin, that enchantment by concepts of carnality, which has engaged a certain type of man, to the exclusion of all other notions, since the dawn of history. The remote ancestors of our Puritan-Philistines of today are to be met with in the Old Testament and the New, and their nearer grandfathers clamoured against the snares of the flesh in all the councils of the Early Church. Not only Western Christianity has had to reckon with them: they have brothers today among the Mohammedan Sufi and in obscure Buddhist sects, and they were the chief preachers of the Russian Raskol, or Reformation. "The Ironsides of Cromwell and the Puritans of New England," says Heard, in his book on the Russian church, "bear a strong resemblance to the Old Believers." But here, in the main, we have asceticism more than Puritanism, as it is now visible; here the sinner combated is chiefly the one within. How are we to account for the wholesale transvaluation of values that came after the Civil War, the transfer of ire from the Old Adam to the happy rascal across the street, the sinister rise of a new Inquisition in the midst of a growing luxury that even the Puritans themselves succumbed to? The answer is to be sought, it seems to me, in the direction of the Golden Calf—in the direction of the fat fields of our Midlands, the full nets of our lakes and coasts, the factory smoke of our cities—even in the direction of Wall Street, that devil's chasm. In brief, Puritanism has become bellicose and tyrannical by becoming rich. The will to power has been aroused to a high flame by an increase in the available draught and fuel, as militarism is engendered and nourished by the presence of men and materials. Wealth, discovering its power, has reached out its long arms to grab the distant and innumerable sinner; it has gone down into its deep pockets to pay for his costly pursuit and flaying; it has created the Puritan *entrepreneur*, the daring and imaginative organizer of Puritanism, the baron of moral endeavour, the invincible prophet of new austerities. And, by the same token, it has issued its letters of marque to the Puritan mercenary, the professional hound of heaven, the moral *Junker*, the Comstock, and out of his skill at his trade there has arisen the whole machinery, so complicated and so effective, of the new Holy Office.

Poverty is a soft pedal upon all branches of human activity, not excepting the spiritual, and even the original Puritans, for all their fire, felt its throttling caress. I think it is Bill Nye who has humorously pictured their arduous life: how they had to dig clams all winter that they would have strength enough to plant corn, and how they had to hoe corn all summer that they would have strength enough to dig clams. That low ebb of fortune worked against the full satisfaction of their zeal in two distinct ways. On the one hand, it kept them but ill-prepared for the cost of offensive enterprise: even their occasional missionarying raids upon the Indians took too much productive energy from their business with the corn and the clams. And on the other hand, it kept a certain restraining humility in their hearts, so that for every Quaker they hanged, they let a dozen go. Poverty, of course, is no discredit, but at all events, it is a subtle criticism. The man oppressed by material wants is not in the best of moods for the more ambitious forms of moral adventure. He not only lacks the means; he is also deficient in the self-assurance, the sense of superiority, the secure and lofty point of departure. If he is haunted by notions of the sinfulness of his neighbours, he is apt to see some of its worst manifestations within himself, and that disquieting discovery will tend to take his thoughts from the other fellow. It is by no arbitrary fiat, indeed, that the brothers of all the expiatory orders are vowed to poverty. History teaches us that wealth, whenever it has come to them by chance, has put an end to their soul-searching. The Puritans of the elder generations, with few exceptions, were poor. Nearly all Americans, down to the Civil War, were poor. And being poor, they subscribed to a *Sklavenmoral*. That is to say, they were spiritually humble. Their eyes were fixed, not upon the abyss below them, but upon the long and rocky road ahead of them.

Their moral passion spent most of its force in self-accusing, self-denial and self-scourging. They began by howling their sins from the mourners' bench; they came to their end, many of them, in the supreme immolation of battle.

But out of the War came prosperity, and out of prosperity came a new morality, to wit, the *Herrenmoral.* Many great fortunes were made in the War itself; an uncountable number got started during the two decades following. What is more, this material prosperity was generally dispersed through all classes: it affected the common workman and the remote farmer quite as much as the actual merchant and manufacturer. Its first effect, as we all know, was a universal cockiness, a rise in pretensions, a comforting feeling that the Republic was a success, and with it, its every citizen. This change made itself quickly obvious, and even odious, in all the secular relations of life. The American became a sort of braggart playboy of the western world, enormously sure of himself and ludicrously contemptuous of all other men. And on the ghostly side there appeared the same accession of confidence, the same sure assumption of authority, though at first less self-evidently and offensively. The religion of the American thus began to lose its inward direction; it became less and less a scheme of personal salvation and more and more a scheme of pious derring-do. The revivals of the 70's had all the bounce and fervour of those of half a century before, but the mourners' bench began to lose its standing as their symbol, and in its place appeared the collection basket. Instead of accusing himself, the convert volunteered to track down and bring in the other fellow. His enthusiasm was not for repentance, but for what he began to call service. In brief, the national sense of energy and fitness gradually superimposed itself upon the national Puritanism, and from that marriage sprung a keen *Wille zur Macht*, a lusty will to power.[1] The American Puritan, by now, was not content with the rescue of his own soul; he felt an irresistible impulse to hand salvation on, to disperse and multiply it, to ram it down reluctant throats, to make it free, universal and compulsory. He had the men, he had the guns and he had the money too. All that was needed was organization. The rescue of the unsaved could be converted into a wholesale business, unsentimentally and economically conducted, and with all the usual aids to efficiency, from skilful sales management to se-

[1] *Cf.* The Puritan, by Owen Hatteras, *The Smart Set*, July, 1916; and The Puritan's Will to Power, by Randolph S. Bourne, *The Seven Arts*, April, 1917.

ductive advertising, and from rigorous accounting to the diligent shutting off of competition.

Out of that new will to power came many enterprises more or less futile and harmless, with the "institutional" church at their head. Piety was cunningly disguised as basketball, billiards and squash; the sinner was lured to grace with Turkish baths, lectures on foreign travel, and free instructions in stenography, rhetoric and double-entry book-keeping. Religion lost all its old contemplative and esoteric character, and became a frankly worldly enterprise, a thing of balance-sheets and ponderable profits, heavily capitalized and astutely manned. There was no longer any room for the spiritual type of leader, with his white choker and his interminable fourthlies. He was displaced by a brisk gentleman in a "business suit" who looked, talked and thought like a seller of Mexican mine stock. Scheme after scheme for the swift evangelization of the nation was launched, some of them of truly astonishing sweep and daring. They kept pace, step by step, with the mushroom growth of enterprise in the commercial field. The Y. M. C. A. swelled to the proportions of a Standard Oil Company, a United States Steel Corporation. Its hugh buildings began to rise in every city; it developed a swarm of specialists in new and fantastic moral and social sciences; it enlisted the same gargantuan talent which managed the railroads, the big banks and the larger national industries. And beside it rose the Young People's Society of Christian Endeavour, the Sunday-school associations and a score of other such grandiose organizations, each with its seductive baits for recruits and money. Even the enterprises that had come down from an elder and less expansive day were pumped up and put on a Wall Street basis: the American Bible Society, for example, began to give away Bibles by the million instead of by the thousand, and the venerable Tract Society took on the feverish ardour of a daily newspaper, even of a yellow journal. Down into our own day this trustification of pious endeavour has gone on. The Men and Religion Forward Movement proposed to convert the whole country by 12 o'clock noon of such and such a day; the Order of Gideons plans to make every traveller read the Bible (American Revised Version!) whether he will or not; in a score of cities there are committees of opulent devotees who take half-pages in the newspapers, and advertise the Decalogue and the Beatitudes as if they were commodities of trade.

Thus the national energy which created the Beef Trust and the Oil Trust achieved equal marvels in the field of religious organization and by exactly the same methods. One needs be no psychologist to perceive in all this a good deal less actual religious zeal than mere lust for staggering accomplishment, for empty bigness, for the unprecedented and the prodigious. Many of these great religious enterprises, indeed, soon lost all save the faintest flavour of devotion—for example, the Y. M. C. A., which is now no more than a sort of national club system, with its doors open to any one not palpably felonious. (I have drunk cocktails in Y. M. C. A. lamaseries, and helped fallen lamas to bed.) But while the war upon godlessness thus degenerated into a secular sport in one direction, it maintained all its pristine quality, and even took on a new ferocity in another direction. Here it was that the lamp of American Puritanism kept on burning; here, it was, indeed, that the lamp became converted into a huge bonfire, or rather a blast-furnace, with flames mounting to the very heavens, and sinners stacked like cordwood at the hand of an eager black gang. In brief, the new will to power, working in the true Puritan as in the mere religious sportsman, stimulated him to a campaign of repression and punishment perhaps unequalled in the history of the world, and developed an art of militant morality as complex in technique and as rich in professors as the elder art of iniquity.

If we take the passage of the Comstock Postal Act, on March 3, 1873, as a starting point, the legislative stakes of this new Puritan movement sweep upward in a grand curve to the passage of the Mann and Webb Acts, in 1910 and 1913, the first of which ratifies the Seventh Commandment with a salvo of artillery, and the second of which put the overwhelming power of the Federal Government behind the enforcement of the prohibition laws in the so-called "dry" States. The mind at once recalls the salient campaigns of this war of a generation: first the attack upon "vicious" literature, begun by Comstock and the New York Society for the Suppression of Vice, but quickly extending to every city in the land; then the long fight upon the open gambling house, culminating in its practical disappearance; then the recrudesence of prohibition, abandoned at the outbreak of the Civil War, and the attempt to enforce it in a rapidly growing list of States; then the successful onslaught upon the Louisiana lottery, and upon its swarm of rivals and successors; then the gradual stamping-out of horse-racing, until finally but two or three States permitted it, and the consequent attack upon the pool-room; then the rise of a theatre-censorship in most of the large cities, and of a moving picture censorship following it; then the revival of Sabbatarianism, with the Lord's Day Alliance, a Canadian invention, in the van; then the gradual tightening of the laws against sexual irregularity, with the unenforceable New York Adultery Act as a typical product; and lastly, the general ploughing up and emotional discussion of sexual matters, with compulsory instruction in "sex hygiene" as its mildest manifestation and the mediaeval fury of the vice crusade as its worst. Differing widely in their targets, these various Puritan enterprises had one character in common: they were all efforts to combat immorality with the weapons designed for crime. In each of them there was a visible effort to erect the individual's offence against himself into an offence against society. Beneath all of them there was the dubious principle—the very determining principle, indeed, of Puritanism—that it is competent for the community to limit and condition the private acts of its members, and with it the inevitable corollary that there are some members of the community who have a special talent for such legislation, and that their arbitrary fiats are, and of a right ought to be, binding upon all.

§ 4

This is the essential fact of the new Puritanism; its recognition of the moral expert, the professional sinhound, the virtuoso of virtue. Under the original Puritan theocracy, as in Scotland, for example, the chase and punishment of sinners was a purely ecclesiastical function, and during the slow disintegration of the theocracy the only change introduced was the extension of that function to lay helpers, and finally to the whole body of laymen. This change, however, did not materially corrupt the ecclesiastical quality of the enterprise: the leader in the so-called militant field still remained the same man who led in the spiritual field. But with the capitalization of Puritan effort there came a radical overhauling of method. The secular arm, as it were, conquered as it helped. That is to say, the special business of forcing sinners to be good was taken away from the preachers and put into the hands of laymen trained in its technique and mystery, and there it remains. The new Puritanism has created an army of gladiators who are not only distinct from the hierarchy, but who, in many instances, actually command and intimidate the hierarchy. This is conspicuously evident in the case of the Anti-Saloon League, an enormously effective fighting organization, with a large staff of highly accomplished experts in its service. These experts do not wait for ecclesiastical support, nor even ask for it; they force it. The clergyman who presumes to protest against their war upon the saloon, even upon the quite virtuous ground that it is not effective enough, runs a risk of condign and merciless punishment. So plainly is this understood, indeed, that in more than one State the clergy of the Puritan denominations openly take orders from these specialists in excoriation, and court their favour without shame. Here a single moral enterprise, heavily capitalized and carefully officered, has engulfed the entire Puritan movement, and a part has become more than the whole.[1]

In a dozen other directions this tendency to transform a religious business into a purely secular business, with lay backers and lay officers, is plainly visible. The increasing wealth of Puritanism has not only augmented its scope and its daring, but it has also had the effect of attracting clever men, of

[1] An instructive account of the organization and methods of the Anti-Saloon League, a thoroughly typical Puritan engine, is to be found in Alcohol and Society, by John Koren; New York, Henry Holt & Co., 1916.

no particular spiritual enthusiasm, to its service. Moral endeavour, in brief, has become a recognized trade, or rather a profession, and there have appeared men who pretend to a special and enormous knowledge of it, and who show enough truth in their pretension to gain the unlimited support of Puritan capitalists. The vice crusade, to mention one example, has produced a large crop of such self-constituted experts, and some of them are in such demand that they are overwhelmed with engagements. The majority of these men have wholly lost the flavour of sacerdotalism. They are not pastors, but detectives, statisticians and mob orators, and not infrequently their secularity becomes distressingly evident. Their aim, as they say, is to do things. Assuming that "moral sentiment" is behind them, they override all criticism and opposition without argument, and proceed to the business of dispersing prostitutes, of browbeating and terrorizing weak officials, and of forcing legislation of their own invention through City Councils and State Legislatures. Their very cocksureness is their chief source of strength. They combat objection with such violence and with such a devastating cynicism that it quickly fades away. The more astute politicians, in the face of so ruthless a fire, commonly profess conversion and join the colours, just as their brethren went over to prohibition in the "dry" States, and the newspapers seldom hold out much longer. The result is that the "investigation" of the social evil becomes an orgy, and that the ensuing "report" of the inevitable "vice commission" is made up of two parts sensational fiction and three parts platitude. Of all the vice commissions that have sat of late in the United States, not one has done its work without the aid of these singularly confident experts, and not one has contributed an original and sagacious idea, nor even an idea of ordinary common sense, to the solution of the problem.

I need not go on piling up examples of this new form of Puritan activity, with its definite departure from a religious foundation and its elaborate development as an everyday business. The impulse behind it I have called a *Wille zur Macht*, a will to power. In terms more homely, it was described by John Fiske as "the disposition to domineer," and in his usual unerring way, he saw its dependence on the gratuitous assumption of infallibility. But even stronger than the Puritan's belief in his own inspiration is his yearning to make some one jump. In other words, he has an ineradicable liking for cruelty in him: he is a sportsman even before he is a moralist, and very often his blood-lust leads him into lamentable excesses. The various vice crusades afford innumerable cases in point. In one city, if the press dispatches are to be believed, the proscribed women of the Tenderloin were pursued with such ferocity that seven of them were driven to suicide. And in another city, after a campaign of repression so unfortunate in its effects that there were actually protests against it by clergymen elsewhere, a distinguished (and very friendly) connoisseur of such affairs referred to it ingenuously as more fun "than a fleet of aeroplanes." Such disorderly combats with evil, of course, produce no permanent good. It is a commonplace, indeed, that a city is usually in worse condition after it has been "cleaned up" than it was before, and I need not point to New York, Los Angeles and Des Moines for the evidence as to the social evil, and to any large city, East, West, North, South, for the evidence as to the saloon. But the Puritans who finance such enterprises get their thrills, not out of any possible obliteration of vice, but out of the galloping pursuit of the vicious. The new Puritan gives no more serious thought to the rights and feelings of his quarry than the gunner gives to the rights and feelings of his birds. From the beginning of the prohibition campaign, for example, the principle of compensation has been violently opposed, despite its obvious justice, and a complaisant judiciary has ratified the Puritan position. In England and on the Continent that principle is safeguarded by the fundamental laws, and during the early days of the anti-slavery agitation in this country it was accepted as incontrovertible, but if any American statesman were to propose today that it be applied to the license-holder whose lawful franchise has been taken away from him arbitrarily, or to the brewer or distiller whose costly plant has been rendered useless and valueless, he would see the days of his statesmanship brought to a quick and violent close.

But does all this argue a total lack of justice in the American character, or even a lack of common decency? I doubt that it would be well to go so far in accusation. What it does argue is a tendency to put moral considerations above all other considerations, and to define morality in the narrow Puritan sense. The American, in other words, thinks that the sinner has no rights that any one is bound to respect, and he is prone to mistake an unsupported charge of sinning, provided it be made violently enough, for actual proof and confession. What is more, he takes an intense joy in the mere chase: he has the true Puritan taste for an *auto da fé* in him. "I am ag'inst capital punishment," said Mr. Dooley, "but we won't get rid av it so long as the people enjie it so much." But though he is thus an eager spectator, and may even be lured into taking part in the pursuit, the average American is not disposed to initiate it, nor to pay for it. The larger Puritan enterprises of today are not popular in the sense of originating in the bleachers, but only in the sense of being applauded from the bleachers. The burdens of the fray, both of toil and of expense, are always upon a relatively small number of men. In a State rocked and racked by a war upon the saloon, it was recently shown, for example, that but five per cent. of the members of the Puritan denominations contributed to the war-chest. And yet the Anti-Saloon League of that State was so sure of support from below that it presumed to stand as the spokesman of the whole Christian community, and even ventured to launch excommunications upon contumacious Christians, both lay and clerical, who objected to its methods. Moreover, the great majority of the persons included in the contributing five per cent. gave no more than a few cents a year. The whole support of the League devolved upon a dozen men, all of them rich and all of them Puritans of purest ray serene. These men supported a costly organization for their private entertainment and stimulation. It was their means of recreation, their sporting club. They were willing to spend a lot of money to procure good sport for themselves—*i.e.*, to procure the best crusading talent available—and they were so successful in that endeavour that they enchanted the populace too, and so shook the State.

Naturally enough, this organization of Puritanism upon a business and sporting basis has had a tendency to attract and create a type of "expert" crusader whose determination to give his employers a good show is uncontaminated by any consideration for the public welfare. The result has been a steady increase of scandals, a constant collapse of moral organizations, a frequent unveiling of whited sepulchres. Various observers have sought to direct the public attention to this significant corruption of the new Puritanism. The New York *Sun*, for example, in the course of a protest against the appointment of a vice commission for New York, has denounced the paid agents of private reform organizations as "notoriously corrupt, undependable and dishonest," and the Rev. Dr. W. S. Rainsford, supporting the charge, has borne testimony out of his own wide experience to their lawlessness, their absurd pretensions to special knowledge, their habit of manufacturing evidence, and their devious methods of shutting off criticism.

But so far, at all events, no organized war upon them has been undertaken, and they seem to flourish more luxuriantly year after year. The individual whose common rights are invaded by such persons has little chance of getting justice, and less of getting redress. When he attempts to defend himself he finds that he is opposed, not only by a financial power that is ample for all purposes of the combat and that does not shrink at intimidating juries, prosecuting officers and judges, but also by a shrewdness which shapes the laws to its own uses, and takes full advantage of the miserable cowardice of legislatures. The moral gladiators, in brief, know the game. They come before a legislature with a bill ostensibly designed to cure some great and admitted evil, they procure its enactment by scarcely veiled insinuations that all who stand against it must be apologists for the evil itself, and then they proceed to extend its aims by bold inferences, and to dragoon the courts into ratifying those inferences, and to employ it as a means of persecution, terrorism and blackmail. The history of the Mann Act offers a shining example of this purpose. It was carried through Congress, over the veto of President Taft, who discerned its extravagance, on the plea that it was needed to put down the traffic in prostitutes; it is enforced today against men who are no more engaged in the traffic in prostitutes than you or I. Naturally enough, the effect of this extension of its purposes, against which its author has publicly protested, has been to make it a truly deadly weapon in the hands of professional Puritans and of denouncers of delinquency even less honest. "Blackmailers of both sexes have arisen," says Mr. Justice McKenna, "using the terrors of the construction now sanctioned by the [Supreme] Court as a help—indeed, the means—for their brigandage. The result is grave and should give us pause." [1]

But that is as far as objection has yet gone; the majority of the learned jurist's colleagues swallowed both the statute and its consequences.[2] There is, indeed, no sign as yet of any organized war upon the alliance between the blackmailing Puritan and the pseudo-Puritan blackmailer. It must wait until a sense of reason and justice shows itself in the American people, strong enough to overcome their prejudice in favour of the moralist on the one hand, and their delight in barbarous pursuits and punishments on the other. I see but faint promise of that change today.

[1] U. S. Rep., vol. 242, No. 7, p. 502.

[2] The majority opinion, written by Mr. Justice Day, is given in U. S. Rep., vol. 242, no. 7, pp. 482-496.

§ 5

I have gone into the anatomy and physiology of militant Puritanism because, so far as I know, the inquiry has not been attempted before, and because a somewhat detailed acquaintance with the forces behind so grotesque a manifestation as comstockery, the particular business of the present essay, is necessary to an understanding of its workings, and of its prosperity, and of its influence upon the arts. Save one turn to England or to the British colonies, it is impossible to find a parallel for the astounding absolutism of Comstock and his imitators in any civilized country. No other nation has laws which oppress the arts so ignorantly and so abominably as ours do, nor has any other nation handed over the enforcement of the statutes which exist to agencies so openly pledged to reduce all aesthetic expression to the service of a stupid and unworkable scheme of rectitude. I have before me as I write a pamphlet in explanation of his aims and principles, prepared by Comstock himself and presented to me by his successor. Its very title is a sufficient statement of the Puritan position: "MORALS, Not Art or Literature." [1] The capi-

[1] New York, (1914).

tals are in the original. And within, as a sort of general text, the idea is amplified: "It is a question of peace, good order and morals, and not art, literature or science." Here we have a statement of principle that, at all events, is at least quite frank. There is not the slightest effort to beg the question; there is no hypocritical pretension to a desire to purify or safeguard the arts; they are dismissed at once as trivial and degrading. And jury after jury has acquiesced in this; it was old Anthony's boast, in his last days, that his percentage of convictions, in 40 years, had run to 98.5.[1]

Comstockery is thus grounded firmly upon that profound national suspicion of the arts, that truculent and almost unanimous Philistinism, which I have described. It would be absurd to dismiss it as an excrescence, and untypical of the American mind. But it is typical, too, in the manner in which it has gone beyond that mere partiality to the accumulation of a definite power, and made that

[1] I quote from page 157 of Anthony Comstock, Fighter, the official biography. On page 239 the number of his prosecutions is given as 3,646, with 2,682 convictions, which works out to but 73 per cent. He is credited with having destroyed 50 tons of books, 28,425 pounds of stereotype plates, 16,900 photographic negatives, and 3,984,063 photographs—enough to fill "sixteen freight cars, fifteen loaded with ten tons each, and the other nearly full."

power irresponsible and almost irresistible. It was Comstock himself, in fact, who invented the process whereby his followers in other fields of moral endeavour have forced laws into the statute books upon the pretence of putting down John Doe, an acknowledged malefactor, and then turned them savagely upon Richard Roe, a peaceable, well-meaning and hitherto law-abiding man. And it was Comstock who first capitalized moral endeavour like baseball or the soap business, and made himself the first of its kept professors, and erected about himself a rampart of legal and financial immunity which rid him of all fear of mistakes and their consequences, and so enabled him to pursue his jehad with all the advantages in his favour. He was, in brief, more than the greatest Puritan gladiator of his time; he was the Copernicus of a quite new art and science, and he devised a technique and handed down a professional ethic that no rival has been able to better.

The whole story is naïvely told in "Anthony Comstock, Fighter," [1] a work which passed under the approving eye of the old war horse himself and is full of his characteristic pecksniffery.[2] His

[1] By Charles Gallaudet Trumbull; New York, Fleming H. Revell Co. (1913).

[2] An example: "All the evil men in New York cannot harm

beginnings, it appears, were very modest. When he arrived in New York from the Connecticut hinterland, he was a penniless and uneducated clodhopper, just out of the Union army, and his first job was that of a porter in a wholesale dry-goods house. But he had in him several qualities of the traditional Yankee which almost always insure success, and it was not long before he began to make his way. One of these qualities was a talent for bold and ingratiating address; another was a vast appetite for thrusting himself into affairs, a yearning to run things—what the Puritan calls public spirit. The two constituted his fortune. The second brought him into intimate relations with the newly-organized Young Men's Christian Association, and led him to the discovery of a form of moral endeavour that was at once novel and fascinating—the unearthing and denunciation of "im-

a hair of my head, were it not the will of God. If it be His will, what right have I or any one to say aught? I am only a speck, a mite, before God, yet not a hair of my head can be harmed unless it be His will. Oh, to live, to feel, to be—Thy will be done!" (pp. 84-5). Again: "I prayed that, if my bill might not pass, I might go back to New York submissive to God's will, feeling that it was for the best. I asked for forgiveness and asked that my bill might pass, if possible; but over and above all, that the will of God be done" (p. 6). Nevertheless, Comstock neglected no chance to apply his backstairs pressure to the members of both Houses.

moral" literature. The first, once he had attracted attention thereby, got him the favourable notice, and finally the unlimited support, of the late Morris K. Jesup, one of the earliest and perhaps the greatest of the moral *entrepreneurs* that I have described. Jesup was very rich, and very eager to bring the whole nation up to grace by *force majeure.* He was the banker of at least a dozen grandiose programs of purification in the seventies and eighties. In Comstock he found precisely the sort of field agent that he was looking for, and the two presently constituted the most formidable team of professional reformers that the country had ever seen.

The story of the passage of the Act of Congress of March 3, 1873,[1] under cover of which the Comstock Society still carries on its campaigns of snouting and suppression, is a classical tale of Puritan impudence and chicanery. Comstock, with Jesup and other rich men backing him financially and politically,[2] managed the business. First, a number of spectacular raids were made on the publishers of such pornographic books as "The Memoirs of Fanny Hill" and "Only a Boy."

[1] Now, with amendments, sections 211, 212 and 245 of the United States Criminal Code.

[2] *Vide* Anthony Comstock, Fighter, pp. 81, 85, 94.

Then the newspapers were filled with inflammatory matter about the wide dispersal of such stuff, and its demoralizing effects upon the youth of the republic. Then a committee of self-advertising clergymen and "Christian millionaires" was organized to launch a definite "movement." And then a direct attack was made upon Congress, and, to the tune of fiery moral indignation, the bill prepared by Comstock himself was forced through both houses. All opposition, if only the opposition of inquiry, was overborne in the usual manner. That is to say, every Congressman who presumed to ask what it was all about, or to point out obvious defects in the bill, was disposed of by the insinuation, or even the direct charge, that he was a covert defender of obscene books, and, by inference, of the carnal recreations described in them. We have grown familiar of late with this process: it was displayed at full length in the passage of the Mann Act, and again when the Webb Act and the Prohibition Amendment were before Congress. In 1873 its effectiveness was helped out by its novelty, and so the Comstock bill was rushed through both houses in the closing days of a busy session, and President Grant accommodatingly signed it.

Once it was upon the books, Comstock made further use of the prevailing uproar to have himself appointed a special agent of the Postoffice Department to enforce it, and with characteristic cunning refused to take any salary. Had his job carried a salary, it would have excited the acquisitiveness of other virtuosi; as it was, he was secure. As for the necessary sinews of war, he knew well that he could get them from Jesup. Within a few weeks, indeed, the latter had perfected a special organization for the enforcement of the new statute, and it still flourishes as the New York Society for the Suppression of Vice; or, as it is better known, the Comstock Society. The new Federal Act, dealing only with the mails, left certain loopholes; they were plugged up by fastening drastic amendments upon the New York Code of Criminal Procedure—amendments forced through the legislature precisely as the Federal Act had been forced through Congress.[1] With these laws in his hands Comstock was ready for his career. It was his part of the arrangement to supply the thrills of the chase; it was Jesup's part to find the money. The partnership kept up until the death of Jesup, in 1908, and after that Comstock readily found new backers. Even his own death, in 1915, did not materially alter a scheme of things which offered such admi-

[1] Now sections 1141, 1142 and 1143 of the Penal Laws of New York.

rable opportunities for the exercise of the Puritan love of spectacular and relentless pursuit, the Puritan delusion of moral grandeur and infallibility, the Puritan will to power.

Ostensibly, as I have said, the new laws were designed to put down the traffic in frankly pornographic books and pictures—a traffic which, of course, found no defenders—but Comstock had so drawn them that their actual sweep was vastly wider, and once he was firmly in the saddle his enterprises scarcely knew limits. Having disposed of "The Confessions of Maria Monk" and "Night Life in Paris," he turned to Rabelais and the Decameron, and having driven these ancients under the book-counters, he pounced upon Zola, Balzac and Daudet, and having disposed of these too, he began a *pogrom* which, in other hands, eventually brought down such astounding victims as Thomas Hardy's "Jude the Obscure" and Harold Frederic's "The Damnation of Theron Ware." All through the eighties and nineties this ecstatic campaign continued, always increasing in violence and effectiveness. Comstock became a national celebrity; his doings were as copiously reported by the newspapers as those of P. T. Barnum or John L. Sullivan. Imitators sprang up in all the larger cities: there was hardly a public library in the land that did not begin feverishly expurgating its shelves; the publication of fiction, and particularly of foreign fiction, took on the character of an extra hazardous enterprise. Not, of course, that the reign of terror was not challenged, and Comstock himself denounced. So early as 1876 a national organization demanding a reasonable amendment of the postal laws got on its legs; in the late eighties "Citizen" George Francis Train defied the whirlwind by printing the Old Testament as a serial; many indignant victims, acquitted by some chance in the courts, brought suit against Comstock for damages. Moreover, an occasional judge, standing out boldly against the usual intimidation, denounced him from the bench; one of them, Judge Jenkins, accused him specifically of "fraud and lying" and other "dishonest practices."[1] But the spirit of American Puritanism was on his side. His very extravagances at once stimulated and satisfied the national yearning for a hot chase, a good show—and in the complaints of his victims, that the art of letters was being degraded, that the country was made ridiculous, the newspaper-reading populace could see no more than an affectation. The reform organization of 1876 lasted but five

[1] U. S. *vs.* Casper, reported in the *Twentieth Century,* Feb. 11, 1892.

years; and then disbanded without having accomplished anything; Train was put on trial for "debauching the young" with an "obscene" serial; [1] juries refused to bring in punitive verdicts against the master showman.

In carrying on this way of extermination upon all ideas that violated their private notions of virtue and decorum, Comstock and his followers were very greatly aided by the vagueness of the law. It prohibited the use of the mails for transporting all matter of an "obscene, lewd, lascivious . . . or filthy" character, but conveniently failed to define these adjectives. As a result, of course, it was possible to bring an accusation against practically *any* publication that aroused the comstockian blood-lust, however innocently, and to subject the persons responsible for it to costly, embarrassing and often dangerous persecution. No man, said Dr. Johnson, would care to go on trial for his life once a week, even if possessed of absolute proofs of his innocence. By the same token, no man

[1] The trial court dodged the issue by directing the jury to find the prisoner not guilty on the ground of insanity. The necessary implication, of course, was that the publication complained of was actually obscene. In 1895, one Wise, of Clay Center, Kansas, sent a quotation from the Bible through the mails, and was found guilty of mailing obscene matter. See The Free Press Anthology, compiled by Theodore Schroeder; New York, Truth Seeker Pub. Co., 1909, p. 258.

wants to be arraigned in a criminal court, and displayed in the sensational newspapers, as a purveyor of indecency, however strong his assurance of innocence. Comstock made use of this fact in an adroit and characteristically unconscionable manner. He held the menace of prosecution over all who presumed to dispute his tyranny, and when he could not prevail by a mere threat, he did not hesitate to begin proceedings, and to carry them forward with the aid of florid proclamations to the newspapers and ill concealed intimidations of judges and juries.

The last-named business succeeded as it always does in this country, where the judiciary is quite as sensitive to the suspicion of sinfulness as the legislative arm. A glance at the decisions handed down during the forty years of Comstock's chief activity shows a truly amazing willingness to accommodate him in his pious enterprises. On the one hand, there was gradually built up a court-made definition of obscenity which eventually embraced almost every conceivable violation of Puritan prudery, and on the other hand the victim's means of defence were steadily restricted and conditioned, until in the end he had scarcely any at all. This is the state of the law today. It is held in the leading cases that anything is obscene which may excite "impure thoughts" in "the minds . . . of persons that are susceptible to impure thoughts,"[1] or which "tends to deprave the minds" of any who, because they are "young and inexperienced," are "open to such influences"[2]—in brief, that anything is obscene that is not fit to be handed to a child just learning to read, or that may imaginably stimulate the lubricity of the most foul-minded. It is held further that words that are perfectly innocent in themselves—"words, abstractly considered, [that] may be free from vulgarism"—may yet be assumed, by a friendly jury, to be likely to "arouse a libidinous passion . . . in the mind of a modest woman." (I quote exactly! The court failed to define "modest woman.")[3] Yet further, it is held that any book is obscene "which is unbecoming, immodest. . . ."[4] Obviously, this last decision throws open the door to endless imbecilities, for its definition merely begs the question, and so makes a reasonable solution ten times harder. It is in such mazes that the Comstocks safely lurk. Almost any printed allusion to sex may be argued

[1] U. S. *vs.* Bennett, 16 Blatchford, 368-9 (1877).

[2] *Idem*, 362; People *vs.* Muller, 96 N. Y., 411; U. S. *vs.* Clark, 38 Fed. Rep. 734.

[3] U. S. *vs.* Moore, 129 Fed., 160-1 (1904).

[4] U. S. *vs.* Heywood, judge's charge, Boston, 1877. Quoted in U. S. *vs.* Bennett, 16 Blatchford.

against as unbecoming in a moral republic, and once it is unbecoming it is also obscene.

In meeting such attacks the defendant must do his fighting without weapons. He cannot allege in his defence that the offending work was put forth for a legitimate, necessary and decent purpose; [1] he cannot allege that a passage complained of is from a standard work, itself in general circulation; [2] he cannot offer evidence that the person to whom a book or picture was sold or exhibited was not actually depraved by it, or likely to be depraved by it; [3] he cannot rest his defence on its lack of such effect upon the jurymen themselves; [4] he cannot plead that the alleged obscenity, in point of fact, is couched in decent and unobjectionable language; [5] he cannot plead that the same or a similar work has gone unchallenged elsewhere; [6] he cannot argue that the circulation of works of the same class has

1 U. S. *vs.* Slenker, 32 Fed. Rep., 693; People *vs.* Muller, 96 N. Y. 408-414; Anti-Vice Motion Picture Co. *vs.* Bell, reported in the *New York Law Journal*, Sept. 22, 1916; Sociological Research Film Corporation *vs.* the City of New York, 83 Misc. 815; Steele *vs.* Bannon, 7 L. R. C. L. Series, 267; U. S. *vs.* Means, 42 Fed. Rep. 605, etc.

2 U. S. *vs.* Cheseman, 19 Fed. Rep., 597 (1884).

3 People *vs.* Muller, 96 N. Y., 413.

4 U. S. *vs.* Bennett, 16 Blatchford, 368-9.

5 U. S. *vs.* Smith, 45 Fed. Rep. 478.

6 U. S. *vs.* Bennett, 16 Blatchford, 360-1; People vs. Berry, 1 N. Y., Crim. R., 32.

set up a presumption of toleration, and a tacit limitation of the definition of obscenity.[1] The general character of a book is not a defence of a particular passage, however unimportant; if there is the slightest descent to what is "unbecoming," the whole may be ruthlessly condemned.[2] Nor is it an admissible defence to argue that the book was not generally circulated, and that the copy in evidence was obtained by an *agent provocateur*, and by false representations.[3] Finally, all the decisions deny the defendant the right to introduce any testimony, whether expert or otherwise, that a book is of artistic value and not pornographic, and that its effect upon normal persons is not pernicious. Upon this point the jury is the sole judge, and it cannot be helped to its decision by taking other opinions, or by hearing evidence as to what is the general opinion.

Occasionally, as I have said, a judge has revolted against this intolerable state of the court- and Comstock-made law, and directed a jury to disregard these astounding decisions.[4] In a recent

[1] People *vs.* Muller, 32 Hun., 212-215.

[2] U. S. *vs.* Bennett, 16 Blatchford, 361.

[3] U. S. *vs.* Moore, 16 Fed. Rep., 39; U. S. *vs.* Wright, 38 Fed. Rep., 106; U. S. *vs.* Dorsey, 40 Fed. Rep., 752; U. S. *vs.* Baker, 155 Mass., 287; U. S. *vs.* Grimm, 15 Supreme Court Rep., 472.

[4] Various cases in point are cited in the Brief on Behalf of

New York case Judge Samuel Seabury actually ruled that "it is no part of the duty of courts to exercise a censorship over literary productions."[1] But in general the judiciary has been curiously complaisant, and more than once a Puritan on the bench has delighted the Comstocks by prosecuting their case for them.[2] With such decisions in their hands and such aid from the other side of the bar, it is no wonder that they enter upon their campaigns with impudence and assurance. All the odds are in their favour from the start. They have statutes deliberately designed to make the defence onerous; they are familiar by long experience with all the

Plaintiff in Dreiser *vs.* John Lane Co., App. Div. 1st Dept. N. Y., 1917. I cite a few: People *vs.* Eastman, 188 N. Y., 478; U. S. *vs.* Swearingen, 161 U. S., 446; People *vs.* Tylkoff, 212 N. Y., 197; In the matter of Worthington Co., 62 St. Rep. 116-7; St. Hubert Guild *vs.* Quinn, 64 Misc., 336-341. But nearly all such decisions are in New York cases. In the Federal courts the Comstocks usually have their way.

1 St. Hubert Guild *vs.* Quinn, 64 Misc., 339.

2 For example, Judge Chas. L. Benedict, sitting in U. S. *vs.* Bennett, *op. cit.* This is a leading case, and the Comstocks make much of it. Nevertheless, a contemporary newspaper denounces Judge Benedict for his "intense bigotry" and alleges that "the only evidence which he permitted to be given was on the side of the prosecution." (Port Jervis, N. Y., *Evening Gazette,* March 22, 1879.) Moreover, a juror in the case, Alfred A. Valentine, thought it necessary to inform the newspapers that he voted guilty only in obedience to judicial instructions.

tricks and surprises of the game; they are sheltered behind organizations, incorporated without capital and liberally chartered by trembling legislatures, which make reprisals impossible in case of failure; above all, they have perfected the business of playing upon the cowardice and vanity of judges and prosecuting officers. The newspapers, with very few exceptions, give them ready aid. Theoretically, perhaps, many newspaper editors are opposed to comstockery, and sometimes they denounce it with great eloquence, but when a good show is offered they are always in favour of the showman [1]—and the Comstocks are showmen of undoubted skill. They know how to make a victim jump and writhe in the ring; they have a talent for finding victims who are prominent enough to arrest attention; they shrewdly capitalize the fact that the pursuer appears more heroic than the prey, and the further fact that the newspaper reader is impatient of artistic pretensions and glad to see an artist made ridiculous. And behind them there is always the steady pressure of Puritan prejudice—the Puritan feeling that "immorality" is the blackest of crimes, and that its practitioner has no rights. It was by making use of these elements

[1] *Vide* Newspaper Morals, by H. L. Mencken, the *Atlantic Monthly*, March, 1914.

that Comstock achieved his prodigies, and it is by making use of them that his heirs and assigns keep up the sport today. Their livelihood depends upon the money they can raise among the righteous, and the amount they can raise depends upon the quality of the entertainment they offer. Hence their adept search for shining marks. Hence, for example, the spectacular raid upon the Art Students' League, on August 2, 1906. Hence the artful turning to their own use of the vogue of such sensational dramatists as Eugène Brieux and George Bernard Shaw, and of such isolated plays as "Trilby" and "Sapho." Hence the barring from the mails of the inflammatory report of the Chicago Vice Commission—a strange, strange case of dog eating dog.

But here we have humour. There is, however, no humour in the case of a serious author who sees his work damaged and perhaps ruined by a malicious and unintelligent attack, and himself held up to public obloquy as one with the vendors of pamphlets of flagellation and filthy "marriage guides." He finds opposing him a flat denial of his decent purpose as an artist, and a stupid and ill-natured logic that baffles sober answer.[1] He finds

[1] As a fair specimen of the sort of reasoning that prevails among the consecrated brethren I offer the following extract from an argument against birth control delivered by the

on his side only the half-hearted support of a publisher whose interest in a single book is limited to his profits from it, and who desires above all things to evade a nuisance and an expense. Not a few publishers, knowing the constant possibility of sudden and arbitrary attack, insert a clause in their contracts whereby an author must secure them against damage from any "immoral" matter in his book. They read and approve the manuscript, they print the book and sell it—but if it is unlucky enough to attract the comstockian lightning, the author has the whole burden to bear,[1] and if they

present active head of the New York Society for the Suppression of Vice before the Women's City Club of New York, Nov. 17, 1916:

"Natural and inevitable conditions, over which we can have no control, will assert themselves wherever population becomes too dense. This has been exemplified time after time in the history of the world where over-population has been corrected by manifestations of nature or by war, flood or pestilence. . . . Belgium may have been regarded as an over-populated country. Is it a coincidence that, during the past two years, the territory of Belgium has been devastated and its population scattered throughout the other countries of the world?"

1 For example, the printed contract of the John Lane Co., publisher of Dreiser's The "Genius," contains this provision: "The author hereby guarantees . . . that the work . . . contains nothing of a scandalous, an immoral or a libelous nature." The contract for the publication of The "Genius" was signed on July 30, 1914. The manuscript had been carefully read by representatives of the publisher, and presumably passed as not scandalous or immoral, inasmuch as the publi-

seek safety and economy by yielding, as often happens, he must consent to the mutilation or even the suppression of his work. The result is that a writer in such a situation, is practically beaten before he can offer a defence. The professional book-baiters have laws to their liking, and courts pliant to their exactions; they fill the newspapers with inflammatory charges before the accused gets his day in court; they have the aid of prosecuting officers who fear the political damage of their enmity, and of the enmity of their wealthy and influential backers; above all, they have the command of far more money than any author can hope to muster. Finally, they derive an advantage from two of the most widespread of human weaknesses, the first being envy and the second being fear. When an author is attacked, a good many of his rivals see only a personal benefit in his difficulties,

cation of a scandalous or immoral book would have exposed the publisher to prosecution. About 8,000 copies were sold under this contract. Two years later, in July, 1916, the Society for the Suppression of Vice threatened to begin a prosecution unless the book was withdrawn. It was withdrawn forthwith, and Dreiser was compelled to enter suit for a performance of the contract. The withdrawal, it will be noticed, was not in obedience to a court order, but followed a mere comstockian threat. Yet Dreiser was at once deprived of his royalties, and forced into expensive litigation. Had it not been that eminent counsel volunteered for his defence, his personal means would have been insufficient to have got him even a day in court.

and not a menace to the whole order, and a good many others are afraid to go to his aid because of the danger of bringing down the moralists' rage upon themselves. Both of these weaknesses revealed themselves very amusingly in the Dreiser case, and I hope to detail their operations at some length later on, when I describe that *cause célèbre* in a separate work.

Now add to the unfairness and malignancy of the attack its no less disconcerting arbitrariness and fortuitousness, and the path of the American author is seen to be strewn with formidable entanglements indeed. With the law what it is, he is quite unable to decide *a priori* what is permitted by the national delicacy and what is not, nor can he get any light from the recorded campaigns of the moralists. They seem to strike blindly, unintelligently, without any coherent theory or plan. "Trilby" is assaulted by the united comstockery of a dozen cities, and "The Yoke" somehow escapes. "Hagar Revelly" is made the subject of a double prosecution in the State and Federal courts, and "Love's Pilgrimage" and "One Man" go unmolested. The publisher of Przybyszewski's "Homo Sapiens" is forced to withdraw it; the publisher of Artzibashef's "Sanine" follows it with "The

Breaking Point." The serious work of a Forel is brought into court as pornography, and the books of Havelock Ellis are barred from the mails; the innumerable volumes on "sex hygiene" by tawdry clergymen and smutty old maids are circulated by the million and without challenge. Frank Harris is deprived of a publisher for his "Oscar Wilde: His Life and Confession" by threats of immediate prosecution; the newspapers meanwhile dedicate thousands of columns to the filthy amusements of Harry Thaw. George Moore's "Memoirs of My Dead Life" are bowdlerized, James Lane Allen's "A Summer in Arcady" is barred from libraries, and a book by D. H. Lawrence is forbidden publication altogether; at the same time half a dozen cheap magazines devoted to sensational sex stories attain to hundreds of thousands of circulation. A serious book by David Graham Phillips, published serially in a popular monthly, is raided the moment it appears between covers; a trashy piece of nastiness by Elinor Glyn goes unmolested. Worse, books are sold for months and even years without protest, and then suddenly attacked; Dreiser's "The 'Genius,'" Kreymborg's "Edna" and Forel's "The Sexual Question" are examples. Still worse, what is held to be unobjectionable in one

State is forbidden in another as *contra bonos mores*.[1] Altogether, there is madness, and no method in it. The livelihoods and good names of hard-striving and decent men are at the mercy of the whims of a horde of fanatics and mountebanks, and they have no way of securing themselves against attack, and no redress for their loss when it comes.

§ 6

So beset, it is no wonder that the typical American maker of books becomes a timorous and ineffective fellow, whose work tends inevitably toward a feeble superficiality. Sucking in the Puritan spirit with the very air he breathes, and perhaps burdened inwardly with an inheritance of the actual Puritan stupidity, he is further kept upon the straight path of chemical purity by the very real perils that I have just rehearsed. The result is a literature full of the mawkishness that the late Henry James so often roared against—a literature almost wholly detached from life as men are living it in the world—in George Moore's phrase, a liter-

[1] The chief sufferers from this conflict are the authors of moving pictures. What they face at the hands of imbecile State boards of censorship is described at length by Channing Pollock in an article entitled "Swinging the Censor" in the *Bulletin* of the Authors' League of America for March, 1917.

ature still at nurse. It is on the side of sex that the appointed virtuosi of virtue exercise their chief repressions, for it is sex that especially fascinates the lubricious Puritan mind; but the conventual reticence that thus becomes the enforced fashion in one field extends itself to all others. Our fiction, in general, is marked by an artificiality as marked as that of Eighteenth Century poetry or the later Georgian drama. The romance in it runs to set forms and stale situations; the revelation, by such a book as "The Titan," that there may be a glamour as entrancing in the way of a conqueror of men as in the way of a youth with a maid, remains isolated and exotic. We have no first-rate political or religious novel; we have no first-rate war story; despite all our national engrossment in commercial enterprise, we have few second-rate tales of business. Romance, in American fiction, still means only a somewhat childish amorousness and sentimentality—the love affairs of Paul and Virginia, or the pale adulteries of their elders. And on the side of realism there is an almost equal vacuity and lack of veracity. The action of all the novels of the Howells school goes on within four walls of painted canvas; they begin to shock once they describe an attack of asthma or a steak burning below stairs; they never penetrate beneath the flow of social concealments and urbanities to the passions that actually move men and women to their acts, and the great forces that circumscribe and condition personality. So obvious a piece of reporting as Upton Sinclair's "The Jungle" or Robert Herrick's "Together" makes a sensation; the appearance of a "Jennie Gerhardt" or a "Hagar Revelly" brings forth a growl of astonishment and rage.

In all this dread of free inquiry, this childish skittishness in both writers and public, this dearth of courage and even of curiosity, the influence of comstockery is undoubtedly to be detected. It constitutes a sinister and ever-present menace to all men of ideas; it affrights the publisher and paralyzes the author; no one on the outside can imagine its burden as a practical concern. I am, in moments borrowed from more palatable business, the editor of an American magazine, and I thus know at first hand what the burden is. That magazine is anything but a popular one, in the current sense. It sells at a relatively high price; it contains no pictures or other baits for the childish; it is frankly addressed to a sophisticated minority. I may thus assume reasonably, I believe, that its readers are not sex-curious and itching adolescents, just as my colleague of the *Atlantic Monthly* may assume reasonably that his readers are not Italian immigrants. Nevertheless, as a practical editor, I find that the Comstocks, near and far, are oftener in my mind's eye than my actual patrons. The thing I always have to decide about a manuscript offered for publication, before ever I give any thought to its artistic merit and suitability, is the question whether its publication will be permitted—not even whether it is intrinsically good or evil, moral or immoral, but whether some roving Methodist preacher, self-commissioned to keep watch on letters, will read indecency into it. Not a week passes that I do not decline some sound and honest piece of work for no other reason. I have a long list of such things by American authors, well-devised, well-imagined, well-executed, respectable as human documents and as works of art—but never to be printed in mine or any other American magazine. It includes four or five short stories of the very first rank, and the best one-act play yet done, to my knowledge, by an American. All of these pieces would go into type at once on the Continent; no sane man would think of objecting to them; they are no more obscene, to a normal adult, than his own bare legs. But they simply cannot be printed in the United States, with the law what it is and the courts what they are.

I know many other editors. All of them are in

the same boat. Some of them try to get around the difficulty by pecksniffery more or less open—for example, by fastening a moral purpose upon works of art, and hawking them as uplifting.[1] Others, facing the intolerable fact, yield to it with resignation. And if they didn't? Well, if one of them didn't, any professional moralist could go before a police magistrate, get a warrant upon a simple affidavit, raid the office of the offending editor, seize all the magazines in sight, and keep them impounded until after the disposition of the case. Editors cannot afford to take this risk. Magazines are perishable goods. Even if, after a trial has been had, they are returned, they are worthless save as waste paper. And what may be done with copies found in the actual office of publication may be done too with copies found on news-stands, and not only in one city, but in two, six, a dozen, a hundred. All the costs and burdens of the contest are on the defendant. Let him be acquitted with honour, and invited to dinner by the judge, he has yet lost his property, and the Comstock hiding be-

[1] For example, the magazine which printed David Graham Phillips' Susan Lenox: Her Rise and Fall as a serial prefaced it with a moral encomium by the Rev. Charles H. Parkhurst. Later, when the novel appeared in book form, the Comstocks began an action to have it suppressed, and forced the publisher to bowdlerize it.

hind the warrant cannot be made to pay. In this concealment, indeed, lurk many sinister things—not forgetting personal enmity and business rivalry. The actual complainant is seldom uncovered; Comstockery, taking on a semi-judicial character, throws its chartered immunity around the whole process. A hypothetical outrage? By no means. It has been perpetrated, in one American city or another, upon fully half of the magazines of general circulation published today. Its possibility sticks in the consciousness of every editor and publisher like a recurrent glycosuria.[1]

But though the effects of comstockery are thus abominably insane and irritating, the fact is not to be forgotten that, after all, the thing is no more than an effect itself. The fundamental causes of all the grotesque (and often half-fabulous) phenomena flowing out of it are to be sought in the habits of mind of the American people. They are, as I have shown, besotted by moral concepts, a moral engrossment, a delusion of moral infallibility. In their view of the arts they are still unable to shake off the naïve suspicion of the Fathers.[2] A work of

[1] An account of a typical prosecution, arbitrary, unintelligent and disingenuous, is to be found in Sumner and Indecency, by Frank Harris, in *Pearson's Magazine* for June, 1917, p. 556.

[2] For further discussions of this point consult Art in America, by Aleister Crowley, *The English Review*, Nov., 1913; Life,

the imagination can justify itself, in their sight, only if it show a moral purpose, and that purpose must be obvious and unmistakable. Even in their slow progress toward a revolt against the ancestral Philistinism, they cling to this ethical bemusement: a new gallery of pictures is welcomed as "improving," to hear Beethoven "makes one better." Any questioning of the moral ideas that prevail—the principal business, it must be plain, of the novelist, the serious dramatist, the professed inquirer into human motives and acts—is received with the utmost hostility. To attempt such an enterprise is to disturb the peace—and the disturber of the peace, in the national view, quickly passes over into the downright criminal.

These symptoms, it seems to me, are only partly racial, despite the persistent survival of that third-rate English strain which shows itself so ingenuously in the colonial spirit, the sense of inferiority, the frank craving for praise from home. The race, in truth, grows mongrel, and the protest against that mongrelism only serves to drive in the fact. But a mongrel race is necessarily a race still in the stage of reaching out for culture; it has not

Art and America, by Theodore Dreiser, *The Seven Arts,* Feb., 1917; and The American; His Ideas of Beauty, by H. L. Mencken, *The Smart Set,* Sept., 1913.

yet formulated defensible standards; it must needs rest heavily upon the superstitions that go with inferiority. The Reformation brought Scotland among the civilized nations, but it took Scotland a century and a half to live down the Reformation.[1] Dogmatism, conformity, Philistinism, the fear of rebels, the crusading spirit; these are the marks of an upstart people, uncertain of their rank in the world and even of their direction.[2] A cultured European, reading a typical American critical journal, must needs conceive the United States, says H. G. Wells, as "a vain, garrulous and prosperous female of uncertain age and still more uncertain temper, with unfounded pretensions to intellectuality and an ideal of refinement of the most negative description . . . the Aunt Errant of Christendom."[3] There is always that blushful shyness, that timorous uncertainty, broken by sudden rages, sudden enunciations of impeccable doctrine, sudden runnings amuck. Formalism is the hall-mark of the national culture, and sins against the one are sins against the other. The American is school-mastered out of gusto, out of joy, out of innocence.

[1] *Vide* The Cambridge History of English Literature, vol. XI, p. 225.

[2] The point is discussed by H. V. Routh in The Cambridge History of English Literature, vol. XI, p. 290.

[3] In Boon; New York, George H. Doran Co., 1915.

He can never fathom William Blake's notion that "the lust of the goat is also to the glory of God." He must be correct, or, in his own phrase, he must bust.

Via trita est tutissima. The new generation, urged to curiosity and rebellion by its mounting sap, is rigorously restrained, regimented, policed. The ideal is vacuity, guilelessness, imbecility. "We are looking at this particular book," said Comstock's successor of "The 'Genius,' " "from the standpoint of its harmful effect on female readers of immature mind." [1] To be curious is to be lewd; to know is to yield to fornication. Here we have the mediaeval doctrine still on its legs: a chance word may arouse "a libidinous passion" in the mind of a "modest" woman. Not only youth must be safeguarded, but also the "female," the untrustworthy one, the temptress. "Modest," is a euphemism; it takes laws to keep her "pure." The "locks of chastity" rust in the Cluny Museum; in place of them we have comstockery. . . .

But, as I have said in hymning Huneker, there is yet the munyonic consolation. Time is a great legalizer, even in the field of morals. We have yet no delivery, but we have at least the beginnings of a revolt, or, at all events, of a protest. We have

[1] In a letter to Felix Shay, Nov. 24, 1916.

already reached, in Howells, our Hannah More; in Clemens, our Swift; in Henry James, our Horace Walpole; in Woodberry, Robinson *et al.*, our Cowpers, Southeys and Crabbes; perhaps we might even make a composite and call it our Johnson. We are sweating through our Eighteenth Century, our era of sentiment, our spiritual measles. Maybe a new day is not quite so far off as it seems to be, and with it we may get our Hardy, our Conrad, our Swinburne, our Thoma, our Moore, our Meredith and our Synge.

THE END

INDEX